PAPER BACK LYRICS

COMPLETE LYRICS FOR OVER 185 SONGS

The

1960s

D0250425

HAL•LEONARD®

ISBN-13: 978-1-4234-1193-2
ISBN-10: 1-4234-1193-5

HAL•LEONARD®
CORPORATION
7777 W. BLUEMOUND RD. P.O. BOX 13819 MILWAUKEE, WI 53213

Visit Hal Leonard Online at
www.halleonard.com

CONTENTS

3

Abraham, Martin and John

Words and Music by Richard Holler

recorded by Dion

Has anybody here seen my old friend Abraham?
Can you tell me where he's gone?
He freed a lotta people,
But it seems the good die young,
But I just looked around and he's gone.

Has anybody here seen my old friend John?
Can you tell me where he's gone?
He freed a lotta people,
But it seems the good die young,
But I just looked around and he's gone.

Has anybody here seen my old friend Martin?
Can you tell me where he's gone?
He freed a lotta people,
But it seems the good die young.
But I just looked around and he's gone.

Didn't you love the things they stood for?
Didn't they try to find some good for you and me?
And we'll be free.
Someday soon;
It's gonna be one day.

Has anybody here seen my old friend Bobby?
Can you tell me where he's gone?
I thought I saw him walkin' up over the hill
With Abraham, Martin and John.

All Alone Am I

English Lyric by Arthur Altman
Original Lyric by Jean Ioannidis
Music by M. Hadjidakis

recorded by Brenda Lee

Refrain:
All alone am I,
Ever since your goodbye,
All alone with just the beat of my heart.
People all around,
But I don't hear a sound,
Just the lonely beating of my heart.

No use in holding other hands,
For I'd be holding only emptiness.
No use in kissing other lips,
For I'd be thinking just of your caress.

Refrain Twice

No other voice can say the words
My heart must hear to ever sing again.
The words you used to whisper low,
No other love can ever bring again.

Refrain

All My Loving

Words and Music by John Lennon and Paul McCartney

recorded by The Beatles

Close your eyes and I'll kiss you,
Tomorrow I'll miss you;
Remember I'll always be true.
And then while I'm away,
I'll write home everyday,
And I'll send all my loving to you.

I'll pretend that I'm kissing,
The lips I am missing
And hope that my dreams will come true.
And then while I'm away,
I'll write home everyday,
And I'll send all my loving to you.

All my loving I will send to you,
All my loving. Darling, I'll be true.

Repeat Song

All my loving, all my loving,
Ooh, all my loving I will send to you.

All You Need Is Love

Words and Music by John Lennon and Paul McCartney

recorded by The Beatles

Love, love, love
Love, love, love
Love, love, love.

There's nothing you can do that can't be done,
Nothing you can sing that can't be sung.
It's easy.
There's nothing you can make that can't be made,
No one you can save that can't be saved.
Nothing you can do, but you can learn how to be in time.
It's easy.

All you need is love, all you need is love,
All you need is love, love, love is all you need.
Love, love, love, love, love, love, love, love, love.
All you need is love, all you need is love,
All you need is love, love,
Love is all you need.

There's nothing you can know that isn't known.
Nothing you can see that isn't shown.
Nowhere you can be that isn't where you're meant to be.
It's easy.

All you need is love, all you need is love,
All you need is love, love, love is all you need.
All you need is love (all together now),
All you need is love (everybody),
All you need is love, love,
Love is all you need.

And I Love Her

Words and Music by John Lennon and Paul McCartney

recorded by The Beatles

I give her all my love,
That's all I do.
And if you saw my love,
You'd love her too.
I love her.

She gives me everything,
And tenderly.
The kiss my lover brings,
She brings to me.
And I love her.

A love like ours
Could never die,
As long as I
Have you near me.

Twice:
Bright are the stars that shine,
Dark is the sky.
I know this love of mine
Will never die.
And I love her.

Baby I Need Your Lovin'

Words and Music by Brian Holland, Lamont Dozier and Edward Holland

recorded by The Four Tops, Johnny Rivers

Baby, I need your lovin'. Baby, I need your lovin'.

Although you're never near, your voice I often hear.
Another day, 'nother night, I long to hold you tight,
'Cause I'm so lonely.

Refrain:
Baby, I need your lovin'. Got to have all your lovin'.
Baby, I need your lovin'. Got to have all your lovin'.

Some say it's a sign of weakness for a man to beg.
Then weak I'd rather be, if it means having you to keep,
'Cause lately I've been losing sleep.

Refrain

Lonely nights echo your name.
Oh, sometimes I wonder will I ever be the same?
Oh yeah! When you see me smiling,
You know things have gotten worse.
Any smile you might see has all been rehearsed.

Darling, I can't go on without you.
This emptiness won't let me live without you.
This loneliness inside me, darling, makes me feel half alive.

Refrain

Repeat and Fade:
Got to have all your lovin'.

And When I Die

Words and Music by Laura Nyro

recorded by Blood, Sweat & Tears

I'm not scared of dyin' and I don't really care.
If it's peace you find in dyin',
Well, then let the end be near,
Just bundle up my coffin 'cause it's cold way down there.
I hear that it's cold way down there.
Yeah. Crazy cold way down there.

Refrain:
And when I die and when I'm gone,
There'll be one child born in this world to carry on,
To carry on.

Now troubles are many, they're as deep as a well.
I can swear there ain't no heaven,
But I pray there ain't no hell.
Swear there ain't no heaven and I pray there ain't no hell.
But I'll never know by living, only my dyin' will tell.
Yes, only my dyin' will tell.
Yeah. Only my dyin' will tell.

Refrain

Yeah, yeah.
Give me my freedom for as long as I be.
All I ask of livin' is to have no chains on me.
All I ask of livin' is to have no chains on me.
And all I ask of dyin' is to go naturally.
I only wanna go naturally.
Here I go, ha!
Here comes the devil right behind.

Spoken:
Look out children!

Here he come.
Here he come.
Hey, Don't wanna go by the devil.
Don't wanna go by the demon.
Don't wanna go by Satan.
Don't wanna die uneasy,
Just let me go naturally.

And when I die, and when I'm dead, dead and gone,
There'll be one child born in our world to carry on,
To carry on.
Yeah, yeah.

Be True to Your School

Words and Music by Brian Wilson and Mike Love

recorded by The Beach Boys

When some loud braggart tries to put me down,
And says his school is great,
I tell him right away now what's the matter?
Buddy ain't you heard of my school?
It's number one in the state.

Refrain:
So be true to your school.
Just like you would to your girl or guy.
Be true to your school now,
And let your colors fly.
Be true to your school.

I got a letterman's sweater with the letters in front
I got for football and track.
I'm proud to wear it now,
When I cruise around the other parts of the town.
I got my decal in back.

Refrain

On Friday we'll be jacked up on the football game,
And I'll be ready to fight.
We're gonna smash 'em now.
My girl will be workin' on her pom-poms now,
And she'll be yellin' tonight.

Refrain

So be true to your school. So be true to your school.

(It's A) Beautiful Morning

Words and Music by Felix Cavaliere and Edward Brigati, Jr.

recorded by The Rascals

It's a beautiful morning, Ah!
I think I'll go outside awhile and just smile.
Just take in some clean fresh air 'cause
No sense in staying inside
If the weather's fine and you've got the time
It's your chance to wake up and plan
Another brand new day.

It's a beautiful morning, Ah!
Each bird keeps singing his own song.
So long I've got to be on my way now,
No good just hanging around.
I've got to cover ground, you couldn't keep me down.
It just ain't no good if the sun shines and you're still inside,
Still inside, still inside, oh, oh.

There will be children with robins and flowers
Sunshine caresses each new waking hour.
Seems to me that people keep seeing more and more today
Lead the way, gotta say, it's O.K., gotta say, oh, oh.

Beyond the Sea

Words and Music by Charles Trenet, Albert Lasry and Jack Lawrence

recorded by Bobby Darin

Somewhere beyond the sea,
Somewhere waiting for me,
My lover stands on golden sands
And watches the ships that go sailing.

Somewhere beyond the sea,
He's [She's] there watching for me.
If I could fly like birds on high,
Then straight to his [her] arms
I'd go sailing.

It's far beyond a star;
It's near beyond the moon.
I know beyond a doubt,
My heart will lead me there soon.

We'll meet beyond the shore:
We'll kiss just as before.
Happy we'll be beyond the sea,
And never again I'll go sailing.

Big Girls Don't Cry

Words and Music by Bob Crewe and Bob Gaudio

recorded by The Four Seasons

Big girls don't cry. Big girls don't cry.

Refrain:
Big girls don't cry, they don't cry.
Big girls don't cry. (Who said they don't cry?)

My girl said good-bye, my, oh my,
My girl didn't cry. (I wonder why.)
(Silly boy) Told my girl we had to break up.
(Silly boy) Thought she would call my bluff.
(Silly boy) Then she said to my surprise,
Big girls don't cry.

Refrain Twice

Baby, I was true, I was true.
Baby, I'm a fool. (I'm such a fool.)
(Silly girl) Shame on you, your mama said.
(Silly girl) You're cryin' in bed.
(Silly girl) Shame on you, you told a lie,
Big girls don't cry.

Big girls don't cry, they don't cry.
Big girls don't cry. (That's just an alibi.)
Big girls don't cry.
Big girls don't cry.

Big Bad John

Words and Music by Jimmy Dean

recorded by Jimmy Dean

Every morning at the mine you could see him arrive,
He stood six-foot-six and weighed two-forty-five.
Kinda broad at the shoulder and narrow at the hip,
And everybody knew you didn't give no lip to Big John!

Refrain:
Big John, Big John,
Big Bad John, Big John.

Nobody seemed to know where John called home,
He just drifted into town and stayed all alone.
He didn't say much, a-kinda quiet and shy,
And if you spoke at all, you just said "hi" to Big John!

Somebody said he came from New Orleans,
Where he got in a fight over a Cajun queen.
And a crashing blow from a huge right hand
Sent a Lousiana fellow to the Promised Land. Big John!

Refrain

Then came the day at the bottom of the mine
When a timber cracked and the men started crying.
Miners were praying and hearts beat fast,
And everybody thought that they'd breathed their last, 'cept John.

Through the dust and the smoke of this man-made hell
Walked a giant of a man that the miners knew well.
Grabbed a sagging timber, gave out with a groan,
And like a giant oak tree, just stood there alone. Big John!

Refrain

And with all of his strength he gave a mighty shove;
Then a miner yelled out, "There's a light up above!"
And twenty men scrambled from a would-be grave,
Now there's only one left down there to save—Big John!

With jacks and timbers they started back down,
Then came that rumble way down in the ground,
And smoke and gas belched out of that mine,
Everybody knew it was the end of the line for Big John!

Refrain

Now they never reopened that worthless pit,
They just placed a marble stand in front of it.
These few words are written on that stand:
"At the bottom of this mine lies a big, big man. Big John!"

Refrain

The Birds and the Bees

Words and Music by Herb Newman

recorded by Jewel Akens

Let me tell ya 'bout the birds and the bees
And the flowers and the trees
And the moon up above
And a thing called love.

Let me tell ya 'bout the stars in the sky
And a girl and a guy
And the way they could kiss,
On a night like this.

When I look into your big brown eyes
It's so very plain to see
That it's time you learned about the facts of life
Starting from "A" to "Z."

Let me tell ya 'bout the birds and the bees
And the flowers and the trees
And the moon up above
And a thing called love.

Blue on Blue

Lyric by Hal David
Music by Burt Bacharach

recorded by Bobby Vinton

Refrain:
Blue on blue, heartache on heartache,
Blue on blue, now that we are through.
Blue on blue, heartache on heartache
And I find I can't get over losing you.

I walk along the street we used to walk.
Two by two lovers pass and as they're passing by
I could die 'cause you're not here with me.
Now the trees are bare, there's sadness in the air
And I'm as blue as I can be.

Refrain

Night after lonely night we meet in dreams.
As I run to your side you wait with open arms;
Open arms that now are closed to me.
Through a vale of tears your vision disappears
And I'm as blue as I can be.

Refrain

Blue Velvet

Words and Music by Bernie Wayne and Lee Morris

recorded by Bobby Vinton

She wore blue velvet, bluer than velvet was the night,
Softer than satin was the light from the stars.
She wore blue velvet, bluer than velvet were her eyes,
Warmer than May her tender sighs; love was ours.
Ours, a love I held tightly,
Feeling the rapture grow like a flame burning brightly.
But when she left, gone was the glow of blue velvet.
But in my heart there'll always be,
Precious and warm, a memory through the years,
And I still can see blue velvet through my tears.

Born to Lose

Words and Music by Ted Daffan

recorded by Ray Charles

Born to lose, I've lived my life in vain.
Every dream has only brought me pain.
All my life I've always been so blue.
Born to lose, and now I'm losing you.

Born to lose, it seems so hard to bear,
How I long to always have you near.
You've grown tired and now you say we're through.
Born to lose, and now I'm losin' you.

Born to lose, my every hope is gone.
It's so hard to face that empty dawn.
You were all the happiness I knew.
Born to lose, and now I'm losin' you.

There's no use to dream of happiness,
All I see is only loveliness.
All my life I've always been so blue.
Born to lose, and now I'm losin' you.

Breaking Up Is Hard to Do

Words and Music by Howard Greenfield and Neil Sedaka

recorded by Neil Sedaka

You tell me that you're leaving,
I can't believe it's true.
Girl, there's just no living without you.

Don't take your love away from me.
Don't you leave my heart in misery.
If you go then I'll be blue,
Breaking up is hard to do.

Remember when you held me tight,
And you kissed me all through the night.
Think of all that we've been through,
Breaking up is hard to do.

They say that breaking up is hard to do.
Now I know, I know that it's true.
Don't say that this is the end.
Instead of breaking up,
I wish that we were making up again,
We were making up again.

I beg of you, don't say good-bye;
Can't we give our love a brand new try?
Yeah, come on, babe, let's start anew,
'Cause breaking up is hard to do.

By the Time I Get to Phoenix

Words and Music by Jimmy Webb

recorded by Glen Campbell

By the time I get to Phoenix she'll be risin'
She'll find the note I left hangin' on her door.
She'll laugh when she reads the part that says I'm leavin',
'Cause I've left that girl so many times before.

By the time I make Albuquerque she'll be working'
She'll probably stop at lunch and give me a call.
But she'll just hear that phone keep on ringin',
Off the wall.

By the time I make Oklahoma she'll be sleepin'
She'll turn softly and call my name out low.
And she'll cry just to think I'd really leave her,
'Though time and time I've tried to tell her so,
She just didn't know,
I would really go.

California Dreamin'

Words and Music by John Phillips and Michelle Phillips

recorded by The Mamas & The Papas

All the leaves are brown, and the sky is grey.
I've been for a walk on a winter's day.
I'd be safe and warm, if I was in L. A.
California dreamin' on such a winter's day.

Stopped into a church, I passed along the way.
Oh, I got down on my knees, and I pretend to pray.
You know the preacher likes the cold. He knows I'm gonna stay.
California dreamin' on such a winter's day.

All the leaves are brown, and the sky is grey.
I've been for a walk on a winter's day.
If I didn't tell her I could leave today.
California dreamin' on such a winter's day.
(California dreamin') on such a winter's day.
(California dreamin') on such a winter's day.

California Girls

Words and Music by Brian Wilson and Mike Love

recorded by The Beach Boys

Well, east coast girls are hip,
I really dig those styles they wear;
And the southern girls with the way they talk,
They knock me out when I'm down there.
The midwest farmer's daughters
Really make you feel alright,
And northern girls, with the way they kiss,
They keep their boyfriends warm at night.

Refrain:
I wish they all could be California,
I wish they all could be California,
I wish they all could be California girls.

The west coast has the sunshine,
And the girls all get so tanned;
I dig a French bikini on Hawaii islands,
Dolls by a palm tree in the sand.
I been all around this great big world,
And I've seen all kinds of girls,
But I couldn't wait to get back in the States,
Back to the cutest girls in the world.

Refrain

Repeat and Fade:
I wish they all could be California...

Call Me

Words and Music by Tony Hatch

recorded by California Chris Montez

If you're feeling sad and lonely,
There's a service I can render.
Tell the one who loves you only,
I can be so warm and tender.

Refrain:
Call me!
Don't be afraid; you can call me.
Maybe it's late, but just call me.
Tell me and I'll be around.

When it seems your friends desert you,
There's somebody thinking of you.
I'm the one who'll never hurt you.
Maybe that's because I love you.

Refrain

Now don't forget me, 'cause if you let me,
I will always stay by you.
You gotta trust me; that's how it must be.
There's so much that I can do.

If you call, I'll be right with you.
You and I should be together.
Take this love I long to give you,
I'll be at your side forever.

Refrain

Call Me Irresponsible

Words by Sammy Cahn
Music by James Van Heusen

from the Paramount Picture *Papa's Delicate Condition*
a standard recorded by various artists

Call me irresponsible,
Call me unreliable,
Throw in undependable too.

Do my foolish alibis bore you?
Well, I'm not too clever.
I just adore you.

Call me unpredictable,
Tell me I'm impractical,
Rainbows I'm inclined to pursue.

Call me irresponsible,
Yes, I'm unreliable,
But it's undeniably true,
I'm irresponsibly mad for you!

Can't Help Falling in Love

Words and Music by George David Weiss, Hugo Peretti and Luigi Creatore

from the Paramount Picture *Blue Hawaii*
recorded by Elvis Presley

Wise men say only fools rush in,
But I can't help falling in love with you.
Shall I stay?
Would it be a sin?
If I can't help falling in love with you.

Like a river flows,
Surely to the sea.
Darling so it goes,
Some things are meant to be.

Take my hand, take my whole life too,
For I can't help falling in love with you.
For I can't help falling in love with you.

Can't Take My Eyes Off of You

Words and Music by Bob Crewe and Bob Gaudio

recorded by Frankie Valli

You're just too good to be true,
Can't take my eyes off of you.
You'd be like heaven to touch,
I wanna hold you so much.
At long last love has arrived,
And I thank God I'm alive.
You're just too good to be true,
Can't take my eyes off of you.

Pardon the way that I stare,
There's nothing else to compare.
The sight of you leaves me weak,
There are no words left to speak.
But if you feel like I feel,
Oh please let me know that it's real.
You're just too good to be true,
Can't take my eyes off of you.

I love you, baby, and if it's quite all right,
I need you, baby, to warm the lonely night.
I love you, baby, trust in my when I say,
Oh, pretty baby, don't bring me down, I pray.
Oh pretty baby, now that I've found you, stay,
And let me love you, baby. Let me love you.

Repeat Song

Repeat and Fade:
I love you, baby, and if it's quite all right,
I need you, baby, to warm the lonely night.
I love you, baby, trust in my when I say,

Cherish

Words and Music by Terry Kirkman

recorded by The Association

Cherish is the word I use to describe
All the feeling that I have hiding here for you inside.
You don't know how many times
I've wished that I had told you.
You don't know how many times
I've wished that I could hold you.
You don't know how many times
I've wished that I could mold you into someone
Who could cherish me as much as I cherish you.

Perish is the word that more than applies
To the hope in my heart each time I realize
That I am not gonna be the one
To share your dreams.
That I am not gonna be the one

To share your schemes.
That I am not gonna be the one
To share what seems to be the life
That you could cherish as I do yours.

Oh, I'm beginning to think
That man has never found
The words that could make you want me.
That have the right amount of letters,
Just the right sound,
That could make you hear, make you see
That you are driving me out of my mind.

Oh, I could say I need you,
But then you'd realize
That I want you,
Just like a thousand other guys
Who'd say they loved you
With all the rest of their lies.
When all they wanted was to touch your face, your hands
And gaze into your eyes.

Repeat Verse 1

And I do cherish you.
And I do cherish you.
Cherish is the word.

Come Together

Words and Music by John Lennon and Paul McCartney

recorded by The Beatles

Here come old flat top.
He come grooving up slowly.
He got joo joo eyeball.
He one holy roller.
He got hair down to his knee.
Got to be a joker he just do what you please.

He wear no shoe shine.
He got toe jam football.
He got monkey finger.
He shoot Coca-Cola.
He say I know you, you know me.
One thing I can tell you is you got to be free.
Come together right now over me.

He bag production.
He got walrus gumboot.
He got Ono sideboard.
He one spinal cracker.
He got feet down below his knee.
Hold you in his armchair you can feel his disease.
Come together right now over me.

He roller coaster.
He got early warning.
He got Muddy Water.
He one Mojo filter.
He say, "One and one and one is three."
Got to be good looking 'cause he so hard to see.
Come together right now over me.
Come together.

Crying in the Chapel

Words and Music by Artie Glenn

recorded by Elvis Presley

You saw me crying in the chapel,
The tears I shed were tears of joy.
I know the meaning of contentment;
Now I am happy with the Lord.
Just a plain and simple chapel
Where humble people go to pray;
I pray the Lord that I'll grow stronger
As I live from day to day.

I've searched and I've searched but I couldn't find
No way on earth to gain peace of mind.
Now I'm happy in the chapel,
Where people are of one accord.
We gather in the chapel
Just to sing and praise the Lord.

Every sinner looks for something
That will put his heart at ease;
There is only one true answer,
He must get down on his knees.
Meet your neighbor in the chapel,
Join with him in tears of joy;
You'll know the meaning of contentment,
Then you'll be happy with the Lord.

You'll search and you'll search but you'll never find
No way on earth to gain peace of mind.
Take your troubles to the chapel,
Get down on your knees and pray;
Your burdens will be lighter
And you'll surely find the way.

Cradle of Love

Words and Music by Jack Fautheree and Wayne Gray

recorded by Johnny Preston

Well, rock-a-bye baby in the treetop;
When the wind blows the cradle will rock.
So rock-a-bye baby in the treetop,
When the wind blows.

Well, Jack be nimble, Jack be quick.
Jack jumped over the candlestick.
He jumped so high up above,
He landed in the cradle of love.

Refrain:
Well, rock-a-bye baby in the treetop;
When the wind blows the cradle will rock.
So rock-a-bye baby in the treetop,
When the wind blows.

Hi diddle diddle, the cat and the fiddle,
The cow jumped over the moon.
And on her way down she met a turtle dove,
Said let's go rockin' in the cradle of love.

Refrain

Jack and Jill went up the hill
To get a pail of water,
Jack fell for Jill and gave her a shove
And landed in the cradle of love.

Refrain

Crying

Words and Music by Roy Orbison and Joe Melson

recorded by Roy Orbison

I was alright for a while
I could smile for a while
But I saw you last night,
You held my hand real tight
As you stopped to say, "Hello."
Oh, you wished me well,
You couldn't tell that I'd been

Crying over you.
Crying over you.
When you said, "So long,"
Left me standing all alone,
Alone and crying,
Crying, crying, crying.
It's hard to understand,
But the touch of your hand
Can start me crying.

I thought that I was over you,
But it's true, so true;
I love you even more than I did before.
But darling, what can I do?
For you don't love me
And I'll always be

Crying over you,
Crying over you.
Yes, now you're gone,
And from this moment on,
I'll be crying
Crying, crying, crying.
It's hard to understand,
But the touch of your hand
Can start me crying,
Yeah, crying, crying over you.

Cycles

Words and Music by Gayle Caldwell

recorded by Frank Sinatra

So I'm down, and so, I'm out,
But, so are many others.
So, I feel like tryin'
To hide my head 'neath these covers.

Life is like the seasons,
After Winter comes the Spring.
So, I'll keep this smile awhile,
And see what tomorrow brings.

I've been told, and I believe
That life is meant for livin'.
Even when my chips are low,
There's still some left for givin'.

I've been many places;
Maybe not as far as you.
So, I think I'll stay awhile,
And see if some dreams come true.

There isn't much that I have learned
Through all my foolish years;
Except that life keeps runnin' in cycles;
First there's laughter: Then, there's tears.

But I'll keep my head up high,
Although I'm kind-a tired.
My gal [man] just up and left last week:
Friday, I got fired.

You know it's almost funny,
But, things can't get worse than now.
So, I'll keep on tryin' to sing,
But please, just don't ask me how.

Daddy's Home

Words and Music by James Sheppard and William H. Miller

recorded by Shep & The Limelites

You're my love, you're my angel,
You're the girl of my dreams.
I'd like to thank you for waiting patiently.
Daddy's home. Daddy's home to stay.

How I waited for this moment to be by your side!
Your best friend's around and told me
You had teardrops in your eyes.
Daddy's home. Daddy's home to stay.

It wasn't on a Sunday, Monday and Tuesday went by.
It wasn't on a Tuesday afternoon. All I could do was cry.
But I made a promise that you treasure, I made it back all to you.
How I waited for this moment to be by your side!

Your best friend's around and told me
You had teardrops in your eyes.
Daddy's home. Daddy's home to stay.

Darling, Be Home Soon

Words and Music by John Sebastian

recorded by The Lovin' Spoonful

Come, and talk of all the things we did today.
Hear, and laugh about our funny little ways.
While we have a few minutes to breathe,
Then I know that it's time you must leave.

Refrain:
But darling be home soon.
I couldn't stand to wait an extra minute if you dawdled.
My darling, be home soon.
It's not just these few hours, but I've been waitin' since I toddled
For the great relief of having you to talk to.

And now a quarter of my life is almost past.
I think I've come to see myself at last,
And I see that the time spent confused
Was the time that I spent without you.
And I feel myself in bloom.

Refrain

Go, and beat your crazy head against the sky.
Try and see behind the houses in your eyes.
It's okay to shoot the moon.

Refrain

Daydream

Words and Music by John Sebastian

recorded by The Lovin' Spoonful

What a day for a daydream,
What a day for a daydreamin' boy.
And I'm lost in a daydream,
Dreamin' 'bout my bundle of joy.
And even if time ain't really on my side,
It's one of those days for taking a walk outside.
I'm blowing the day to take a walk in the sun,
And fall on my face on somebody's new mown lawn.

I've been having a sweet dream,
I've been dreamin' since I woke up today.
It's starring me and my sweet dream,
'Cause she's the one makes me feel this way.

And even if time is passing by a lot,
I couldn't care less about the dues you say I got.
Tomorrow I'll pay the dues for dropping my load,
And fall on my face on somebody's sleepy bull-toad.

And you be sure that if you're feelin' right,
A daydream will last till long into the night.
Tomorrow at breakfast you may prick up your ears,
Or you may be daydreamin' for a thousand years.

What a day for a daydream,
Custom made for a daydreamin' boy.
And I'm lost in a daydream,
Dreamin' 'bout my bundle of joy.

Daydream Believer

Words and Music by John Stewart

recorded by The Monkees

Oh, I could hide 'neath the wings
Of the bluebird as she sings;
The six o'clock alarm would never ring.
But it rings and I rise,
Wipe the sleep out of my eyes.
My shaving razor's cold and it stings.

Refrain:
Cheer up, sleepy Jean.
Oh, what can it mean,
To a daydream believer
And a homecoming queen?

You once thought of me
As a white knight on his steed.
Now you know how happy you can be.
Oh, and our good times start and end
Without dollar one to spend,
But how much, baby, do we really need?

Refrain Twice

Dedicated to the One I Love

Words and Music by Lowman Pauling and Ralph Bass

recorded by The Mamas & The Papas, The Shirelles

While I'm far away from you, my baby,
I know it's hard for you, my baby,
Because it's hard for me, my baby.
And the darkest hour is just before dawn.
Each night before you go to bed, my baby,
Whisper a little prayer for me, my baby.
And then tell all the stars above.
This is dedicated to the one I love.

Life can never be exactly like I want it to be,
I could be satisfied knowing you love me.
There's one thing I want you to do especially for me,
And it's something that everybody needs.

While I'm far away from you, my baby,
Whisper a little prayer for me, my baby.
Because it's hard for me, my baby.
And the darkest hour is just before dawn.
There's one thing I want you to do especially for me,
And it's something everybody needs.

Each night before you go to bed, my baby,
Whisper a little prayer for me, my baby.
And then tell all the stars above.
This is dedicated to the one I love.

Repeat and Fade:
Dedicated to the one I love. Dedicated to the one I love.

Did You Ever Have to Make Up Your Mind?

Words and Music by John Sebastian

recorded by The Lovin' Spoonful

Did you ever have to make up your mind
And pick up on one and leave the other behind?
It's not often easy and not often kind.
Did you ever have to make up your mind?

Did you ever have to finally decide
And say yes to one and let the other one ride?
There's so many changes and tears you must hide.
Did you ever have to finally decide?

Sometimes there's one with big blue eyes, cute as a bunny,
With hair down to here and plenty of money.
And just when you think she's that one in the world
Your heart gets stolen by some mousy little girl.

And then you know you better make up your mind
And pick up on one and leave the other behind.
It's not often easy and not often kind.
Did you ever have to make up your mind?

Sometime you really dig a girl the moment you kiss her,
And then you get distracted by her older sister,
When in walks her father and takes you in line
And says, "You better go home, son, and make up your mind."

Then you better finally decide
And say yes to one and let the other one ride.
There's so many changes and tears you must hide.
Did you ever have to finally decide?

Do Wah Diddy Diddy

Words and Music by Jeff Barry and Ellie Greenwich

recorded by Manfred Mann

There he was, just a-walkin' down the street, singin'
Do wah diddy diddy down diddy do.
Poppin' his fingers and a-shuffling his feet, singin'
Do wah diddy diddy down diddy do.
He looked good (yeah, yeah).
He looked fine (yeah, yeah).
He looked good, he looked fine,
And I nearly lost my mind.

Before I knew it he was walkin' next to me, singin'
Do wah diddy diddy down diddy do.
He took my hand, just as nat'ral as can be, singin'
Do wah diddy diddy down diddy do.
We walked on (yeah, yeah)
To my door (yeah, yeah).
We walked on to my door,
And he stayed a little more.

My, my, my, my,
I knew we were fallin' in love.
My, my, my, my,
I told him all the things I was dreamin' of.

Now we're together nearly every single day, singin'
Do wah diddy diddy down diddy do.
We're so happy, and that's how we're gonna stay, singin'
Do wah diddy diddy down diddy do.

'Cause I'm his (yeah, yeah),
And he's mine (yeah, yeah).
Well, I'm his and he's mine,
And the weddin' bells will chime, singin'
Do wah diddy diddy down diddy do.
Do wah diddy diddy down diddy do.

Do You Believe in Magic

Words and Music by John Sebastian

recorded by The Lovin' Spoonful

Do you believe in magic, in a young girl's heart,
How music can free her whenever it starts.
And it's magic if the music is groovy,
It makes you feel happy like an old-time movie.
I'll tell you 'bout the magic and a-free your soul,
But it's like tryin' to tell a stranger 'bout rock and roll.

If you believe in magic don't bother to choose,
If it's jug band music or rhythm and blues.
Just go and listen, it'll start with a smile
That won't wipe off your face no matter how hard you try.
Your feet will start tappin' and you can't seem to find,
How you got there so just blow your mind.

If you believe in magic come along with me,
We'll dance until morning 'til there's just you and me.
And maybe, if the music is right
I'll meet you tomorrow sort of late at night.
And we'll go dancin' baby then you'll see,
How the magic's in the music and music's in me.
Yeah!

Repeat and Fade:
Do you believe like I believe?
Do you believe like I believe?

Don't Let the Sun Catch You Crying

Words and Music by Gerard Marsden, Fred Marsden,
Les Chadwick and Les Maguire

recorded by Gerry & The Pacemakers

Don't let the sun catch you crying
The night's the time for all your tears.
Your heart may be broken tonight,
But tomorrow in the morning light
Don't let the sun catch you crying.

The nighttime shadows disappear
And with them go all your tears.
For the morning will bring joy
For every girl and boy.
So, don't let the sun catch you crying.

We know that crying's not a bad thing
But stop your crying when the birds sing.

It may be hard to discover
That you've been left for another.
But don't forget that life's a game
And it always comes again.
Oh, don't let the sun catch you crying.

Don't let the sun catch you crying
Oh no, oh oh oh.

(Sittin' On) The Dock of the Bay

Words and Music by Steve Cropper and Otis Redding

recorded by Otis Redding

Sittin' in the morning sun,
I'll be sittin' when the evenin' come.
Watchin' the ships roll in,
Then I watch 'em roll away again.
Yeah, I'm sittin' on the dock of the bay,
Watchin' the tide roll away.
Ooh, I'm just sittin' on the dock of the bay,
Wastin' time.

I left my home in Georgia,
Headed for the Frisco bay.
I have nothin' to live for,
Look like nothin's gonna come my way.
So I'm just gonna sit on the dock of the bay,
Watchin' the tide roll away.
Ooh, I'm just sittin' on the dock of the bay,
Wastin' time.

Looks like nothin's gonna change;
Everything still remains the same.
I can't do what ten people tell me to do,
So I guess I'll remain the same.

Sittin' here restin' my bones,
And this loneliness won't leave me alone.
Two thousand miles I roam,
Just to make this dock my home.
Now I'm just gonna sit at the dock of the bay,
Watchin' the tide roll away.
Ooh, I'm just sittin' on the dock of the bay,
Wastin' time.

Downtown

Words and Music by Tony Hatch

recorded by Petula Clark

When you're alone and life is making you lonely
You can always go downtown.
When you've got worries all the noise and the hurry
Seem to help I know, downtown.
Just listen to the music of the traffic in the city.
Linger on the sidewalk where the neon signs are pretty.
How can you lose?

The lights are much brighter there.
You can forget all your troubles,
Forget all your cares so go downtown
Things'll be great when you're downtown.
No finer place for sure, downtown,
Everything's waiting for you.
Downtown.

Don't hang around and let your problems surround you,
There are movie shows, downtown.
Maybe you know some little places to go
To where they never close, downtown.
Just listen to the rhythm of a gentle bossa nova.
You'll be dancing with him too before the night is over.
Happy again.

The lights are much brighter there.
You can forget all your troubles,
Forget all your cares, so go downtown,
Where all the lights are bright.
Downtown, waiting for you tonight.
Downtown, you're gonna be alright now.
Downtown.

Downtown. Downtown. Downtown.
Downtown. Downtown.

And you may find somebody kind to help and understand you;
Someone who is just like you and needs
A gentle hand to guide them along.
So maybe I'll see you there.
We can forget all our troubles, forget all our cares,
So go downtown.
Things'll be great when you're downtown.
Don't wait a minute more. Downtown.
Everything's waiting for you.
Downtown. Downtown. Downtown.
Repeat and Fade: Downtown. Downtown.

Dream Baby
(How Long Must I Dream)

Words and Music by Cindy Walker

recorded by Roy Orbison

Dream baby got me dreamin'
Sweet dreams the whole day through.
Dream baby got me dreamin'
Sweet dreams night time too.
I love you and I'm dreamin' of you.
That won't do.
Dream baby, make me stop my dreamin'.
You can make my dreams come true.

Sweet dream baby,
Sweet dream baby,
Sweet dream baby,
How long must I dream?

Ev'rybody's Somebody's Fool (Everybody's Somebody's Fool)

Words and Music by Jack Keller and Howard Greenfield

recorded by Connie Francis

The tears I cried for you could fill an ocean,
But you don't know how many tears I cry;
And though you only lead me on and hurt me,
I couldn't bring myself to say goodbye.

Refrain:
'Cause everybody's somebody's fool,
Everybody's somebody's plaything,
And there are no exceptions to the rule.
Yes, everybody's somebody's fool.

I told myself it's best that I forget you,
Though I'm a fool at least I know the score;
But, darling, I'd be twice as blue without you.
It hurts, but I'd come running back for more.

Refrain

Some day you'll find someone to really care for,
And if her love should prove to be untrue,
You'll know how much this heart of mine is breaking,
You'll cry for her the way I cried for you. Yes...

Refrain

Eve of Destruction

Words and Music by P.F. Sloan and Steve Barri

recorded by Barry McGuire

The Eastern world, it is explodin',
Violence flarin' and bullets loadin'.
You're old enough to kill, but not for votin',
You don't believe in war, but what's that gun you're totin'?
And even the Jordan River has bodies floatin'!
But you tell me over and over and over again my friend.
Ah, you don't believe we're on the eve of destruction.

Don't you understand what I'm tryin' to say?
Can't you feel the fear that I'm feelin' today?
If the button is pushed there's no running away.
There'll be no one to save with the world in a grave.
Take a look around you, boy,
It's bound to scare you, boy.

My blood's so mad feels like coagulatin',
I'm sittin' here just contemplatin'.
You can't twist the truth it knows no regulatin'
And a handful of senators don't pass legislation.
Marches alone can't bring integration
When human respect is disintegratin'.
This whole crazy world is just too frustratin'.

Think of all the hate there is in Red China
Then take a look around to Selma, Alabama!
You may leave here for four days in space
But when you return, it's the same old place,
The pounding drums, the pride and disgrace.
You can bury your dead, but don't leave a trace.
Hate your next door neighbor, but don't forget to say grace.

You don't believe we're on the eve of destruction.

Ferry 'Cross the Mersey

Words and Music by Gerrard Marsden

recorded by Gerry & The Pacemakers

Life goes on day after day,
Hearts torn in every way.
So ferry 'cross the Mersey
'Cause this land's the place I love
And here I'll stay.

People they rush everywhere
Each with their own secret care.
So ferry 'cross the Mersey
And always take me there,
The place I love.

People around every corner
They seem to smile and say
We don't care what your name is, boy,
We'll never send you away.

So I'll continue to say,
Hope I always will stay.
So ferry 'cross the Mersey
'Cause this land's the place I love
And here I'll stay, and here I'll stay,
Here I'll stay.

The Fool on the Hill

Words and Music by John Lennon and Paul McCartney

recorded by The Beatles

Day after day, alone on a hill,
The man with the foolish grin is keeping perfectly still;
But nobody wants to know him,
They can see that he's just a fool,
And he never gives an answer.
But the fool on the hill sees the sun going down,
And the eyes in his head see the world spinning round.

Well on the way, head in a cloud,
The man of a thousand voices talking perfectly loud;
But nobody ever hears him,
Or the sound he appears to make,
And he never seems to notice.
But the fool on the hill sees the sun going down
And the eyes in his head see the world spinning round.

And nobody seems to like him,
They can tell what he wants to do,
And he never shows his feelings.
But the fool on the hill sees the sun going down
And the eyes in his head see the world spinning round.

He never listens to them,
He knows that they're the fools.
They don't like him.
The fool on the hill sees the sun going down
And the eyes in his head see the world spinning round.

For Once in My Life

Words by Ronald Miller
Music by Orlando Murden

recorded by Stevie Wonder

Goodbye, old friend,
This is the end
Of the man I used to be.
'Cause there's been a strange
And welcome change in me.

For once in my life I have someone who needs me,
Someone I've needed so long.
For once, unafraid, I can go where life leads me
And somehow I know I'll be strong.
For once I can touch what my heart used to dream of
Long before I knew
Someone warm like you
Would make my dream come true.
For once in my life
I won't let sorrow hurt me, not like it's hurt me before.
For once I have something I know won't desert me,
I'm not alone anymore.
For once I can say this is mine, you can't take it,
Long as I know I have love, I can make it.
For once in my life I have someone who needs me.

For once I can feel that somebody's heard my plea.
For once in my life I have someone who needs me.

Gentle on My Mind

Words and Music by John Hartford

recorded by Glen Campbell

It's knowing that your door is always open,
And your path is free to walk,
That makes me tend to leave my sleeping bag,
Rolled up and stashed behind your couch.

And it's knowing I'm not shackled,
By forgotten words and bonds,
And the ink stains that have dried upon some line;
That keeps you in the back-roads
By the rivers of my memory,
That keeps you gentle on my mind.

Fun, Fun, Fun

Words and Music by Brian Wilson and Mike Love

recorded by The Beach Boys

Well, she got her daddy's car
And she cruised through the hamburger stand now.
Seems she forgot all about the library
Like she told her old man now.
And with her radio blastin',
Goes cruising just as fast as she can now.

Refrain:
And she'll have fun, fun, fun,
Till her daddy takes the T-bird away.

Well, the girls can't stand her
'Cause she walks, looks, and drives like an ace now.
She makes the Indy 500
Look like a Roman chariot race now.
A lotta guys try to catch her,
But she leads them on a wild goose chase now.

Refrain

A-well, you knew all along
That your dad was gettin' wise to you now.
And since he took your set of keys
You've been thinking that your fun is all through now.
But you can come along with me,
'Cause we gotta lotta things to do now.

Three Times:
And you'll have fun, fun, fun,
Now that daddy took the T-bird away.

Fun, fun, fun,
Now that daddy took the T-bird away.

Games People Play

Words and Music by Joe South

recorded by Joe South

Oh, the games people play now,
Every night and every day now,
Never meanin' what they say, now,
Never sayin' what they mean.
And they while away the hours
In their ivory towers,
'Til they're covered up with flowers,
In the back of a black limousine.

Refrain:
La, da, da, da, da, da, da.
La, da, da, da, da, da, dee.
Talkin' 'bout you and me,
And the games people play.

Oh, we make one another cry,
Break a heart then we say goodbye,
Cross our hearts and we hope to die,
That the other was to blame.
Neither one will ever give in.
So, we gaze at an eight by ten,
Thinkin' 'bout the things that might have been.
It's a dirty rotten shame.

Refrain

People walkin' up to you,
Singin' "Glory, hallelujah!"
And they're tryin' to sock it to you
In the name of the Lord.
They gonna teach you how to meditate,
Read your horoscope, cheat your fate,
And furthermore, to hell with hate.
Come on get on board.

Refrain

Look around, tell me what you see.
What's happenin' to you and me?
God, grant me the serenity
To remember who I am,
'Cause you're givin' up your sanity
For your pride and your vanity.
Turn your back on humanity
And your don't give a da, da, da,da, da.

Refrain

Go Away, Little Girl

Words and Music by Gerry Goffin and Carole King

recorded by Steve Lawrence

Go away, little girl,
Go away, little girl,
I'm not supposed to be alone with you.
I know that your lips are sweet,
But our lips must never meet.
I belong to someone else and I must be true.

Oh, go away, little girl,
Go away, little girl.
It's hurting me more each minute that you delay.
When you are near me like this,
You're much too hard to resist.
So go away, little girl,
Before I beg you to stay.

God Only Knows

Words and Music by Brian Wilson and Tony Asher

recorded by The Beach Boys

I may not always love you,
But long as there are stars above you;
You never need to doubt it,
I'll make you so sure about it,
God only knows what I'd be without you.

If you should ever leave me,
Oh, life would still go on believe me;
The world could show nothing to me,
So what good would living do me?
God only knows what I'd be without you,
God only knows what I'd be without you,
God only knows.

Goin' Out of My Head

Words and Music by Teddy Randazzo and Bobby Weinstein

recorded by Little Anthony & The Imperials

Well I think I'm going out of my head.
Yes I think I'm going out of my head
Over you, over you.

I want you to want me
I need you so badly,
I can't think of anything but you.

And I think I'm going out of my head.
'Cause I can't explain the tears that I shed
Over you, over you.

I see you each morning;
But you just walk past me,
You don't even know that I exist.

Goin' out of my head over you,
Out of my head over you.
Out of my head day and night,
Night and day and night, wrong or right,

I must think of a way into your heart,
There's no reason why
My being shy should keep us apart.

Repeat and Fade:
And I think I'm going out of my head.
Yes I think I'm going out of my head.

Good Vibrations

Words and Music by Brian Wilson and Mike Love

recorded by The Beach Boys

I, I love the colorful clothes she wears,
And the way the sunlight plays upon her hair.
I hear the sound of a gentle word,
On the wind that lifts her perfume through the air.

Refrain:
I'm thinkin' of good vibrations,
She's giving me the excitations.
Ooh, bop, bop, good vibrations.

Close my eyes. She's somehow closer now,
Softly smile, I know she must be kind.
When I look in her eyes,
She goes with me to a blossom world.

Refrain

Ah, my, my, what elation.
I don't know where, but she sends me there.
My, my, one sensation.
Oh, my, my, what elation.

Three times:
Gotta keep those lovin' good vibrations a-happenin' with her.

Good, good, good, good vibrations.

Green Green Grass of Home

Words and Music by Curly Putman

recorded by Tom Jones, Porter Wagoner

It's good to touch the green, green grass of home.
The old home town looks the same
As I step down from the train,
And there to meet me is my mama and papa.
Down the road I look and there runs Mary,
Hair of gold and lips like cherries.
Its good to touch the green, green grass of home.

Refrain:
Yes, they'll all come to meet me,
Arms reaching, smiling sweetly;
It's good to touch the green, green grass of home.

The old house is still standing
Though the paint is cracked and dry,
And there's that old oak tree that I used to play on.

Down the lane I walk with my sweet Mary,
Hair of gold and lips like cherries.
It's good to touch the green, green grass of home.

Refrain

Spoken:
Then I awake and look around me
At four gray walls that surround me
And I realize that I was only dreaming.

For there's a guard and there's a sad old padre,
Arm in arm we'll walk at daybreak.
Again I'll touch the green, green grass of home.

Yes, they'll all come to see me,
In the shade of that old oak tree
As they lay me 'neath the green, green grass of home.

A Groovy Kind of Love

Words and Music by Toni Wine and Carole Bayer Sager

recorded by The Mindbenders

When I'm feelin' blue,
All I have to do
Is take a look at you,
Then I'm not so blue.
When you're close to me
I can feel your heart beat
I can hear you breathing in my ear.

Refrain:
Wouldn't you agree,
Baby, you and me
Got a groovy kind of love.
We got a groovy kind of love.

Anytime you want to
You can turn me on to
Anything you want to,
Any time at all.
When I taste your lips,
Oh, I start to shiver,
Can't control the quivering inside.

Refrain

When I'm in your arms
Nothing seems to matter
If the world would shatter I don't care.

Refrain

Happy Birthday Sweet Sixteen

Words and Music by Howard Greenfield and Neil Sedaka

recorded by Neil Sedaka

Tonight's the night I've waited for,
Because you're not a baby anymore.
You've turned into the prettiest girl I've ever seen.
Happy birthday sweet sixteen.

What happened to that funny face?
My little tomboy now wears satins and lace.
I can't believe my eyes; you're just a teenage dream.
Happy birthday sweet sixteen.

If I should smile with sweet surprise,
It's just that you've grown up before my very eyes,
You've turned into the prettiest girl I've ever seen.
Happy birthday sweet sixteen.

When you were only six, I was your big brother;
Then when you were ten, we didn't like each other.
When you were thirteen, you were my funny valentine.
But since you've grown up your future is sewn up,
From now on, you're gonna be mine.

Happy Together

Words and Music by Garry Bonner and Alan Gordon

recorded by The Turtles

Imagine me and you, I do.
I think about you day and night,
It's only right
To think about the girl you love,
And hold her tight,
So happy together.

If I should call you up,
Invest a dime,
And you say you belong to me
And ease my mind
Imagine how the world would be,
So very fine,
So happy together.

I can see me lovin' nobody but you
For all my life.
When you're with me baby, the skies will be blue
For all of my life.
Me and you and you and me,
No matter how they toss the dice,
It has to be.

The only one for me is you,
And you for me,
So happy together,
So happy together.

He'll Have to Go

Words and Music by Joe Allison and Audrey Allison

recorded by Jim Reeves, Jeanne Black

Put your sweet lips a little closer to the phone.
Let's pretend that we're together all alone.
I'll tell the man to turn the jukebox way down low.
And you can tell your friend there with you he'll have to go.

Whisper to me, tell me do you love me true,
Or is he holding you the way I do?
Though love is blind, make up your mind, I've got to know.
Should I hang up or will you tell him he'll have to go?

You can't say the words I want to hear
While you're with another man.
If you want me, answer "yes" or "no,"
Darling, I will understand.

Repeat Verse 1

He's So Fine

Words and Music by Ronald Mack

recorded by The Chiffons

Doo lang, doo lang, doo lang,
Doo lang, doo lang.

He's so fine, (doo lang, doo, lang, doo lang)
Wish he were mine, (doo lang, doo, lang, doo lang)
That handsome boy over there (doo lang, doo, lang, doo lang)
The one with the wavy hair. (doo lang, doo, lang, doo lang)

I don't know how I'm gonna do it, (doo lang, doo, lang, doo lang)
But I'm gonna make him mine. (doo lang, doo, lang, doo lang)
Be the envy of all the girls, (doo lang, doo, lang, doo lang)
It's just a matter of time. (doo lang, doo, lang)

He's a soft spoken guy, (doo lang, doo, lang, doo lang)
Also seems kind of shy. (doo lang, doo, lang, doo lang)
Makes me wonder if I (doo lang, doo, lang, doo lang)
Should even give him a try. (doo lang, doo, lang, doo lang)

But then again he can't shy, (doo lang, doo, lang, doo lang)
He can't shy away forever. (doo lang, doo, lang, doo lang)
And I'm gonna make him mine (doo lang, doo, lang, doo lang)
If it takes me forever. (doo lang, doo, lang)

He's so fine. (oh yeah)
Gotta make him mine (oh yeah)
Sooner or later, (oh yeah)
I hope it's not later. (oh yeah)

We got to get together, (oh yeah)
The sooner the better, (oh yeah)
I just can't wait, I just can't wait
To be held in his arms.

If I were a queen (doo lang, doo, lang, doo lang)
And he asked me to leave my throne (doo lang, doo, lang, doo lang)
I'd do anything that he asked, (doo lang, doo, lang, doo lang)
Anything to make him my own. (doo lang, doo, lang, doo lang)

Repeat and Fade:
Oh he's so fine, so fine, so fine, so fine.
He's so fine, so fine, oh yeah, so fine.

Hello, Goodbye

Words and Music by John Lennon and Paul McCartney

recorded by The Beatles

You say yes, I say no,
You say stop, I say go go go.
Oh no.
You say goodbye and I say hello.
Hello, hello, I don't know why you say goodbye, I say hello.
Hello, hello, I don't know why you say goodbye, I say hello.

I say high, you say low.
You say why, and I say I don't know.
Oh no.
You say goodbye and I say hello.
Hello, hello, I don't know why you say goodbye, I say hello.
Hello, hello, I don't know why you say goodbye, I say hello.

Why do you say goodbye, goodbye, bye, bye?
Oh no.
You say goodbye and I say hello.
Hello hello, I don't know why you say goodbye, I say hello.
Hello hello, I don't know why you say goodbye, I say hello.

You say yes, I say no,
(I say yes, but I may mean no.)
You say stop, And I say go, go, go.
(I can stay till it's time to go)
Oh, oh no.
You say goodbye and I say hello.
Hello, hello, I don't know why you say goodbye, I say hello.
Hello, hello, I don't know why you say goodbye, I say hello.
Hello, hello...

Hello Mary Lou

Words and Music by Gene Pitney and C. Mangiaracina

recorded by Ricky Nelson

You passed me by one sunny day,
Flashed those big brown eyes my way,
And, ooh, I wanted you forever more.
I'm not one that gets around,
I swear my feet stuck to the ground,
And though I never did meet you before,

Refrain:
I said, "Hello Mary Lou, good-bye heart.
Sweet Mary Lou, I'm so in love with you.
I knew, Mary Lou, we'd never part.
So hello Mary Lou, goodbye heart."

I saw your lips, I heard your voice,
Believe me I just had no choice.
Wild horses couldn't make me stay away.
I thought about a moonlit night,
My arms about you good an' tight,
That's all I had to see for me to say,

Refrain

Hello Mudduh, Hello Fadduh! (A Letter from Camp)

Words and Music by Allan Sherman and Lou Busch

recorded by Allan Sherman

Hello Mudduh, hello Fadduh,
Here I am at Camp Granada;
Camp is very entertaining,
And they say we'll have some fun
If it stops raining.

I went hiking with Joe Spivy,
He developed poison ivy;
You remember Leonard Skinner?
He got ptomaine poisoning
Last night after dinner.

All the counselors hate the waiters,
And the lake has alligators;
And the head coach wants no sissies,
So he reads to us from
Something called Ulysses.

Now I don't want this should scare ya,
But my bunkmate has malaria;
You remember Jeffrey Hardy?
They're about to organize
A searching party.

Take me home, oh Mudduh, Fadduh take me home,
I hate Granada; don't leave me out in the forest,
Where I might get eaten by a bear.
Take me home, I promise I will not make noise,
Or mess the house with other boys.
Oh please don't make me stay, I've been here one whole day.

Dearest Fadduh, darling Mudduh,
How's my precious little bruddah?
Let me come home if you miss me,
I would even let Aunt Bertha hug and kiss me.

Wait a minute, it stopped hailing,
Guys are swimming, guys are sailing!
Playing baseball, gee, that's better,
Mudduh, Fadduh, kindly disregard this letter.

Hey Jude

Words and Music by John Lennon and Paul McCartney

recorded by The Beatles

Hey Jude, don't make it bad,
Take a sad song and make it better.
Remember to let her into your heart,
Then you can start to make it better.
Hey Jude, don't be afraid.
You were made to go out and get her.
The minute you let her under your skin,
Then you begin to make it better.

And anytime you feel the pain,
Hey Jude, refrain,
Don't carry the world upon your shoulders,
For well you know that it's a fool who plays it cool
By making the world a little colder.

Hey Jude, don't let me down,
You have found her now go and get her.
Remember (Hey Jude) to let her into your heart
Then you can start to make it better.

So let it out and let it in,
Hey Jude, begin,
You're waiting for someone to perform with,
And don't you know that it's just you.
Hey Jude, you'll do.
The movement you need is on your shoulder.

Hey Jude, don't make it bad,
Take a sad song and make it better.
Remember to let her under your skin,
Then you begin to make it better.
Better, better, better...

Honey

Words and Music by Bobby Russell

recorded by Bobby Goldsboro

See the tree, how big it's grown,
But friend, it hasn't been too long it wasn't big.
I laughed at her and she got mad,
The first day that she planted it was just a twig.

Then the first snow came and she ran out
To brush the snow away so it wouldn't die.
Came runnin' in all excited,
Slipped and almost hurt herself, I laughed 'til I cried.

She was always young at heart,
Kind-a dumb and kind-a smart and I loved her so.
I surprised her with a puppy,
Kept me up all Christmas Eve, two years ago.

And it would sure embarrass her
When I came home for working late
'Cause I would know that she's been sittin' there
And cryin' over some sad and silly late, late show.

And Honey, I miss you and I'm being good
And I love to be with you; if only I could.

She wrecked the car and she was sad
And so afraid that I'd be mad, but what the heck.
Though I pretended hard to be
Guess she could say she saw through me and hugged my neck.

I came home unexpectedly
And found her crying needlessly in the middle of the day,
And it was in the early spring,
When flowers bloom and robins sing she went away.

And Honey, I miss you and I'm being good
And I love to be with you; if only I could.

Yes, one day, while I wasn't home,
While she was there and all alone, the angels came.
Now all I have is memories of Honey,
And I wake up nights and call her name.

Now my life's an empty stage,
Where Honey lived and Honey played, and love grew up.
A small cloud passes overhead
And cries down in the flower bed that Honey loved.

How Sweet It Is
(To Be Loved by You)

Words and Music by Edward Holland, Lamont Dozier and Brian Holland

recorded by Marvin Gaye

Refrain:
How sweet it is to be loved by you.
How sweet it is to be loved by you.

I needed the shelter of someone's arms,
There you were.
I needed someone to understand my ups and downs,
There you were.
With sweet love and devotion,
Deeply touching my emotion.
I want to stop and thank you, baby;
I want to stop and thank you, baby, yes I do.

Refrain

I close my eyes at night,
Wonderin' where would I be without you in my life.
Everything I did was just a bore,
Everywhere I went, seems I've been there before.
But you brighten up for me all of my days
With a love so sweet in so many ways.
I want to stop and thank you, baby;
I want to stop and thank you, baby, yes I do.

Refrain

You were better to me than I was to myself.
For me there's you and there ain't nobody else.
I want to stop and thank you, baby;
I want to stop and thank you, baby, yes I do.

Refrain

Hurt So Bad

Words and Music by Teddy Randazzo, Bobby Weinstein and Bobby Hart

recorded by Little Anthony & The Imperials

I know you don't know what I'm going through,
Standing here looking at you.
Well let me tell you that it hurt so bad.
It makes me feel so bad.
It makes me hurt so bad to see you again,
Like needles and pins.

People say you've been makin' out O.K.
She's in love; don't stand in her way.
But let me tell you that it hurt so bad.
It makes me feel so bad.
It's gonna hurt so bad if you walk away.

Why don't you stay and let me make it up to you?
Stay, I'll do anything you want me to.
You loved me before, please love me again.
I can't let you go back to him.
Please don't go, please don't go.

Twice:
It hurt so bad.
Come back, it hurt so bad.
Don't make me hurt so bad,
I'm beggin' you please.
Please don't go.

I Can't Stop Loving You

Words and Music by Don Gibson

recorded by Ray Charles

Those happy hours that we once knew,
Though long ago, still make me blue.
They say that time heals a broken heart,
But time has stood still since we've been apart.

I can't stop loving you,
So I've made up my mind
To live in memory
Of old lonesome times.
I can't stop wanting you,
It's useless to say,
So I'll just live my life
In dreams of yesterday.

Repeat Verse 1

I can't stop loving you,
There's no use to try.
Pretend there's someone new;
I can't live a lie.
I can't stop wanting you
The way that I do.
There's only been one love for me,
That one love is you.

I Can't Help Myself
(Sugar Pie, Honey Bunch)

Words and Music by Brian Holland, Lamont Dozier and Edward Holland

recorded by The Four Tops

Sugar pie, honey bunch,
You know that I love you.
I can't help myself,
I love you and nobody else.

In and out my life
You come and you go,
Leaving just your picture behind
And I kissed it a thousand times.

When you snap your finger or wink your eye
I come a-running to you.
I'm tied to your apron strings
And there's nothing that I can do.

Can't help myself, no I can't help myself.

Sugar pie, honey bunch,
I'm weaker than a man should be.
I can't help myself,
I'm a fool in love you see.

Wanna tell you I don't love you,
Tell you that we're through, and I've tried.
But every time I see your face
I get all choked up inside.

When I call you're name, girl, it starts the flame
Burning in my heart, tearing it apart.
No matter how I try, my love I cannot hide.

Repeat and Fade:
'Cause sugar pie, honey bunch,
You know that I'm weak for you.
Can't help myself, I love you and nobody else.
Sugar pie, honey bunch,
Do anything you ask me to.
Can't help myself, I love you and nobody else.

I Couldn't Live Without Your Love

Words and Music by Tony Hatch and Jackie Trent

recorded by Petula Clark

You're the only one that I rely on,
A shoulder there for me to cry on.
And the hours alone that I'm without you
All I ever do is think about you.
No one knows that you're so understanding
Even though my love is so demanding,
Every time you look at me
then you know we'll both agree
That no other love could be.

Refrain:
I couldn't live without your love,
Now I know you're really mine,
Got to have you all the time.

Didn't like you much when I first met you
But somehow I couldn't quite forget you.
Said you didn't want a friend or lover
That your life was happy with another.
But as time went by my love grew stronger
Knew that I just couldn't wait any longer,
For I couldn't let you go
And I had to tell you so
That I loved then you'd know.

Refrain

Now the tears are gone and I'm not crying
When you say you love me you're not lying,
So if people want to stare
I know I don't really care
Just as long as you are there.

Refrain Twice

I Get Around

Words and Music by Brian Wilson and Mike Love

recorded by The Beach Boys

Refrain:
I get around from town to town.
I'm a real cool head,
I'm makin' real good bread.

I'm gettin' bugged, drivin' up an' down the same ol' strip.
I gotta find a new place where the kids are hip.
My buddies and me are gettin' real well known,
Yeah, the bad guys know us and they leave us alone.

Refrain

We always take my car 'cause it's never been beat.
And we've never missed yet with the girls we meet.
None of the guys go steady 'cause it wouldn't be right,
To leave your best girl home on a Saturday night.

Refrain

I Left My Heart in San Francisco

Words by Douglass Cross
Music by George Cory

recorded by Tony Bennett

The loveliness of Paris
Seems somehow sadly gay,
The glory that was Rome
Is for another day.
I've been terribly alone
And forgotten in Manhattan.
I'm going home
To my city by the bay.

I left my heart
In San Francisco.
High on a hill,
It calls to me.
To be where little cable cars
Climb half-way to the stars!
The morning fog
May chill the air
I don't care!

My love waits there
In San Francisco,
Above the blue and windy sea.
When I come home to you,
San Francisco,
Your golden sun
Will shine for me!

I Got a Woman

Words and Music by Ray Charles and Renald J. Richard

recorded by Jimmy McGriff

I got a woman way over town,
She's good to me, oh yeah!
Well, I got a woman way over town,
She's good to me, oh yeah!
Now she's my dreamboat, oh, yes indeed,
She's just the kind of girl I need.
I found a woman way over town,
She's good to me, oh yeah!

I save my kisses and all my huggin'
Just for her, oh yeah!
I save my kisses and all my huggin'
Just for her, oh yeah!
When I say, "Baby, please take my hand,"

She holds me tight, she's my lover girl.
I found a woman way over town,
She's good to me, oh yeah!

She always answers my beck and call,
Ever-lovin' mama mama tree-top tall.
I feel so proud walkin' by her side,
Couldn't get a better girl,
No matter how hard I tried.

I got a woman way over town,
She's good to me, oh yeah!
Someday we'll marry, way over town,
She's good to me, oh yeah!
Someday we'll marry, don't you understand,
'Cause she's my only lover girl.
I found a woman way over town,
She's good to me, oh yeah!

I Hear a Symphony

Words and Music by Edward Holland, Lamont Dozier and Brian Holland

recorded by The Supremes

You've given me a true love
And every day I thank you love,
For a feeling that's so new,
So inviting, so exciting.
Whenever you are near,
I hear a symphony,
A tender melody pulling me closer,
Closer to your arms.

Then suddenly, ooh, your lips are touching mine.
A feeling so divine 'til I leave the past behind.
I'm lost in a world made for you and me.
Ooh, love me. Whenever you are near I hear a symphony
Play sweet and tenderly every time your lips meet mine baby.

Baby, baby, I feel a joy within.
Don't let this feeling end.
Let it go on and on and on now baby.

Baby, baby, those tears that fill my eyes,
I cry not for myself
But for those who've never felt the joy we've felt.
Whenever you are near, I hear a symphony
Each time you speak to me
I hear a tender rhapsody of love, love.

Baby, baby, as you stand up holding me
Whispering how much you care,
A thousand violins fill the air now.

Baby, baby, don't let this moment end,
Keep standing close to me,
Ooh so close to me, baby baby.

Baby, baby, I hear a symphony,
A tender melody, ah it goes on and on
And on and on…

I Heard It Through the Grapevine

Words and Music by Norman J. Whitfield and Barrett Strong

recorded by Gladys Knight & The Pips, Marvin Gaye

I bet you're wonderin' how I knew
'Bout your plans to make me blue,
With some other guy you knew before.
Between the two of us guys
You know I loved you more.
It took me by surprise I must say
When I found out yesterday.
Don't you know that:

Refrain:
I heard it through the grapevine
Not much longer would you be mine.
Oh, I heard it through the grapevine.
Oh, I'm just about to lose my mind.
Honey, honey oh yeah.

Ooh. I know a man ain't supposed to cry,
But these tears I can't hold inside.
Losin' you would end my life you see,
'Cause you mean that much to me.
You could have told me yourself
That you loved someone else.
Instead:

Refrain

People say believe half of what you see,
Son, and none of what you hear.
But I can't help but be confused.
If it's true, please tell me dear.
Do you plan to let me go
For the other guy you loved before?
Don't you know that:

Refrain

I Know a Place

Words and Music by Tony Hatch

recorded by Petula Clark

Every day when the work is behind you,
And the shop and the store put some lock on the door,
Just get away where your worries won't find you.
If you like, well, I'll tell you more.

Don't let the day get the better of you,
When the evening comes there's so much to do.
You better put on your best and wear a smile,
Just come along with me awhile, 'cause I tell you.

I know a place where the music is fine
And the lights are always low.
I know a place where we can go.

At the door there's a man who will greet you,
Then you go downstairs to some tables and chairs.
Soon I'm sure you'll be tapping your feet,
Because the beat is the greatest there.

All around there are girls and boys,
It's a swingin' place, a cellar full of noise.
It's got an atmosphere of its own somehow,
You've gotta come along right now, 'cause I tell you.

I know a place where the music is fine
And the lights are always low.
I know a place where we can go.

I know a place where we can go.
I know a place where the lights are low.
You're gonna love this place I know.

I Like It Like That

Words and Music by Chris Kenner

Recorded by Chris Kenner, The Dave Clark Five

Refrain (Twice):
Come on, come on, let me show you where it's at!
Come on, come on, let me show you where it's at!
Come on, come on, let me show you where it's at!
The name of the place is "I like it like that."

They got a little place a-down the track.
The name of the place is "I like it like that."
Now, you take Sally, and I'll take Sue,
And we're gonna rock away all our blues.

Refrain

Now the last time I was down there, I lost my shoes.
They had some cat shoutin' the blues.
The people was yelling, shoutin' for more,
And all they kept sayin' was "Go, man, go!"

Refrain

I Love How You Love Me

Words and Music by Barry Mann and Larry Kolber

recorded by The Paris Sisters, Bobby Vinton

I love how you love me.
I love how you kiss me.
And when I'm away from you,
I love how you miss me.
And I love the way
You always treat me tenderly.
But, darling, most of all,
I love how you love me.

I love how your heart beats
Whenever I hold you.
I love how you think of me
Without being told to.
And I love the way your touch
Is almost heavenly.
But, darling, most of all,
I love how you love me.

Repeat Verse 2

I love how you love me.
I love how you love me.
I love how you love me.

I Only Want to Be with You

Words and Music by Mike Hawker and Ivor Raymonde

recorded by Dusty Springfield

I don't know what it is that makes me love you so.
I only know I never wanna let you go,
'Cause you started somethin', oh, can't you see
That ever since we met you've had a hold on me?
It happens to be true. I only want to be with you.

It doesn't matter where you go or what you do,
I wanna spend each moment of the day with you.
Oh, look what has happened with just one kiss.
I never knew that I could be in love like this.
It's crazy but it's true. I only want to be with you.

You stopped and smiled at me,
Asked if I'd care to dance.
I fell into your open arms
And I didn't stand a chance.

No listen, honey, I just wanna be beside you everywhere.
As long as we're together, honey, I don't care
'Cause you started somethin', oh, can't you see
That ever since we met you've had a hold on me?
No matter what you do, I only want to be with you.

I Say a Little Prayer

Lyric by Hal David
Music by Burt Bacharach

recorded by Dionne Warwick

The moment I wake up
Before I put on my make-up
I say a little prayer for you.
While combing my hair now
And wondering what dress to wear now
I say a little prayer for you.

Refrain:
Forever, forever you'll stay in my heart
And I will love you forever and ever.
We never will part.
Oh, how I'll love you.
Together, together, that's how it must be
To live without you
Would only mean heartbreak for me.

I run for the bus, dear,
While riding I think of us, dear.
I say a little prayer for you.
At work I just take time
And all through my coffee break time
I say a little prayer for you.

Refrain

My darling, believe me,
For me there is no one but you.
Please love me too.
I'm in love with you
Answer my prayer.
Say you love me too.

I Second That Emotion

Words and Music by William "Smokey" Robinson and Alfred Cleveland

recorded by Smokey Robinson & The Miracles

Maybe you'll wanna give me kisses sweet,
But only for one night with no repeat.
And maybe you'll go away and never call,
And a taste of honey's worse than none at all.

Refrain:
Oh, little girl, in that case I don't want no part.
I do believe that that would only break my heart.
Oh, but if you feel like lovin' me,
If you got the notion, I second that emotion.
So if you fell like giving me a lifetime of devotion,
I second that emotion.

Maybe you think that love will tie you down
And you don't have the time to hang around.
Or maybe you think that love will make us fools,
And so it makes you wise to break the rules.

Refrain Twice

I Started a Joke

Words and Music by Barry Gibb, Robin Gibb and Maurice Gibb

recorded by Bee Gees

I started a joke, which started the whole world crying.
But I didn't see that the joke was on me.

I started to cry, which started the whole world laughing;
Oh, if I'd only seen that the joke was on me.

I looked at the skies, running my hands over my eyes,
And I fell out of bed, hurting my head from things that I said.

Till I finally died, which started the whole world living;
Oh, if I'd only seen that the joke was on me.
Oh, no, that the joke was on me.

I Want to Hold Your Hand

Words and Music by John Lennon and Paul McCartney

recorded by The Beatles

Oh, yeah, I'll tell you something
I think you'll understand.
When I say that something,
I want to hold your hand,
I want to hold your hand,
I want to hold your hand.

Oh, please say to me
You'll let me be your man,
And please say to me
You'll let me hold your hand.
Now let me hold your hand,
I want to hold your hand.

And when I touch you
I feel happy inside.
It's such a feeling
That my love I can't hide,
I can't hide, I can't hide!

Yeah, you got that something
I think you'll understand.
When I say that something,
I want to hold your hand,
I want to hold your hand,
I want to hold you hand.

And when I touch you
I feel happy inside.
It's such a feeling
That my love I can't hide,
I can't hide, I can't hide!

Yeah, you got that something
I think you'll understand.
When I feel that something,
I want to hold your hand,
I want to hold your hand,
I want to hold your hand,
I want to hold you hand.

I Was Made to Love Her

Words and Music by Stevie Wonder, Lula Mae Hardaway,
Sylvia Moy and Henry Cosby

recorded by Stevie Wonder

I was born in Li'l Rock, had a childhood sweetheart;
We were always hand in hand.
I wore high top shoes and shirt tails, Suzy was in pigtails;
I knew I loved her even then.

You know my papa disapproved it, my mama boo-hooed it,
But I told them time and time again.
"Don't you know I was made to love her, build my world all around
her."
Yeah! Hey, hey, hey.

She's been my inspiration, showed appreciation
For the love I gave her through the years.
Like a sweet magnolia tree, my love blossomed tenderly.
My love grew sweeter through the years.

I know that my baby love me, my baby needs me.
That's why we made it through the years.
I was made to love her, worship and adore her,
Hey, hey, hey.

All through thick and thin our love just won't end,
'Cause I love my baby, love my baby. Ah!

My baby loves me, my baby needs me
And I know I ain't going nowhere.
I was knee-high to a chicken when that love bug bit me.
I had the fever with each passing year.

Or even if the mountain tumbles, if this whole world crumbles,
By her side I'll still be standing there.
'Cause I was made to love her. I was made to live for her.
Yeah! Hey, hey, hey. Ah!

I was made to love her, build my world all around her.
Hey, hey, hey. Oo, baby,
I was made to please her, you know Stevie ain't gonna leave her. No!
Hey, hey, hey. Oo wee, baby, Hey, hey, hey.

I Will Follow Him
(I Will Follow You)

English Words by Norman Gimbel and Arthur Altman
French Words by Jacques Plante
Music by J.W. Stole and Del Roma

recorded by Little Peggy March

I will follow him,
Follow him wherever he may go.
There isn't an ocean too deep,
A mountain so high it can keep me away.

I must follow him.
Ever since he touched my hand I knew
That near him I always must be,
And nothing can keep him from me, he is my destiny.

I love him, I love him, I love him
And where he goes I'll follow, I'll follow, I'll follow.
He'll always be my true love, my true love, my true love,
From now until forever, forever, forever.

I will follow him,
Follow him wherever he may go.
There isn't an ocean too deep,
A mountain so high it can keep, keep me away,
Away from my love.

I love him, I love him, I love him
And where he goes I'll follow, forever and ever
And side by side together I'll be with my true love,
And share a thousand sunsets together beside him.

I will follow him,
Follow him wherever he may go.
There isn't an ocean too deep,
A mountain so high it can keep, keep me away,
Away from my love. Ah.

I'm into Something Good

Words and Music by Gerry Goffin and Carole King

recorded by Herman's Hermits

Woke up this mornin' feelin' fine,
I felt like the world was my valentine.
Last night I met a new boy in the neighborhood,
And something tells me I'm into something good.

He's kind of quiet but not too shy,
And I can tell he's my kind of guy.
He danced every slow dance with me like I hoped he would.
Something tells me I'm into something good.

We only talked for a minute or two,
And I felt like I knew him my whole life through.
I don't know if you can call it love,
But he's everything that I've been dreamin' of.

When he walked me home and he held my hand,
I knew it wouldn't be just a one night stand,
'Cause he asked to see me next week and I told him he could.
Something tells me I'm into something good.

I'm Leaving It Up to You

Words and Music by Don Harris and Dewey Terry, Jr.

Recorded by Dale & Grace

Refrain:
I'm leavin' it all up to you.
You decide what you're gonna do.
Now, do you want my love,
Or are we through?

That's why—

Refrain

I've got my heart in my hand.
I, I, I don't understand,
What have I done wrong?
I worship the ground you walk on

That's why—

Refrain

Or are we through? Or are we through?

I'm Sorry

Words and Music by Ronnie Self and Dub Albritten

recorded by Brenda Lee

I'm sorry, so sorry, that I was such a fool.
I didn't know love could be so cruel.
You tell me mistakes are part of being young,
But that doesn't right the wrong that's been done.
I'm sorry, so sorry; please accept my apology,
But love is blind and I was too blind to see.

I've Told Ev'ry Little Star

Lyrics by Oscar Hammerstein II
Music by Jerome Kern

from *Music in the Air*
recorded by Linda Scott

I make up things to say on my way to you.
On my way to you, I find things to say.
I can write poems too, when you're far away.
When you're far away, I write poems too.
But when you are near, my lips go dry.
When you are near, I only sigh oh, dear.

I've told ev'ry little star,
Just how sweet you are,
Why haven't I told you?
I've told ripples in a brook,
Made my heart an open book.
Why haven't I told you?

Friends ask me, am I in love?
I always answer "Yes."
Might as well confess,
If I don't, they guess.
Maybe you may know it too.
Oh, my darling, if you do,
Why haven't you told me?

If I Had a Hammer
(The Hammer Song)

Words and Music by Lee Hays and Pete Seeger

recorded by Trini Lopez; Peter, Paul & Mary

If I had a hammer,
I'd hammer in the morning,
I'd hammer in the evening
All over this land;
I'd hammer out danger,
I'd hammer out a warning,
I'd hammer out love between
All of my brothers,
All over this land.

If I had a bell,
I'd ring it in the morning,
I'd ring it in the evening
All over this land;
I'd ring out danger,
I'd ring out a warning,
I'd ring out love between
All of my brothers,
All over this land.

If I had a song,
I'd sing it in the morning,
I'd sing it in the evening
All over this land;
I'd sing out danger,
I'd sing out a warning,
I'd sing out love between
All of my brothers,
All over this land.

Well, I got a hammer,
And I've got a bell,
And I've got a song
All over this land;
It's the hammer of justice,
It's the bell of freedom,
It's the song about love between
All of my brothers,
All over this land.

If I Were a Carpenter

Words and Music by Tim Hardin

recorded by Bobby Darin

If I were a carpenter, and you were a lady,
Would you marry me anyway, would you have my baby?
If a tinker were my trade, would you still love me,
Carrying the pots I made, following behind me?

Refrain:
Save my love through loneliness,
Save my love for sorrow,
I've given you my onliness,
Come and give me your tomorrow.

If I worked my hands in wood, would you still love me?
Answer me babe, "Yes I would, I'd put you above me."
If I were a miller, at a mill wheel grinding,
Would you miss your colored box, your soft shoes shining?

Refrain

The Impossible Dream (The Quest)

Lyric by Joe Darion
Music by Mitch Leigh

from *Man of La Mancha*

To dream the impossible dream,
To fight the unbeatable foe,
To bear with unbearable sorrow,
To run where the brave dare not go.

To right the unrightable wrong,
To love pure and chaste from afar,
To try when your arms are too weary,
To reach the unreachable star!

This is my quest,
To follow that star,
No matter how hopeless,
No matter how far;
To fight for the right
Without question or pause.
To be willing to march into hell for a heavenly cause!

And I know,
If I'll only be true
To this glorious quest,
That my heart
Will lie peaceful and calm,
When I'm laid to my rest,

And the world will be better for this;
That one man, scorned and covered with scars,
Still strove with his last ounce of courage,
To reach the unreachable stars.

In My Room

Words and Music by Brian Wilson and Gary Usher

recorded by The Beach Boys

There's a room where I can go and tell my secrets to,
In my room, in my room.
In my room.

In this world I lock out all my worries and my cares,
In my room, in my room.
In my room.

Do my dreaming, and my scheming, lie awake and pray.
Do my crying and my sighing, laugh at yesterday.

Now it's dark and I'm alone, but I won't be afraid;
In my room, in my room, in my room
In my room, in my room, in my room,
In my room.

It's My Party

Words and Music by Herb Wiener, Wally Gold and John Gluck, Jr.

recorded by Lesley Gore

Nobody knows where my Johnny has gone,
But Judy left the same time.
Why was he holding her hand,
When he's supposed to be mine?

Refrain:
It's my party and I'll cry if I want to,
Cry if I want to,
Cry if I want to.
You would cry too, if it happened to you.

Play all my records, keep dancing all night,
But leave me alone for awhile.
'Til Johnny's dancing with me,
I've got no reason to smile.

Refrain

Judy and Johnny just walked through the door,
Like a queen and her king.
Oh, what a birthday surprise,
Judy's wearing his ring.

Refrain

In the Ghetto
(The Vicious Circle)

Words and Music by Mac Davis

recorded by Elvis Presley

As the snow flies
On a cold and grey Chicago mornin',
A poor little baby child is born
In the ghetto.
And his mama cries.
'Cause if there's one thing she don't need
It's another hungry mouth to feed
In the ghetto.

People, don't you understand
The child needs a helping hand
Or he'll grow to be an angry young man some day.
Take a look at you and me
Are we too blind to see?
Or do we simply turn our heads
And look the other way?

Well, the world turns
And a hungry little boy with a runny nose
Plays in the street as the cold wind blows
In the ghetto.
And his hunger burns.

So he starts to roam the streets at night
And he learns how to steal and he learns how to fight
In the ghetto.
And then one night in desperation,
A young man breaks away.

He buys a gun, steals a car,
Tries to run, but he don't get far.
And his mama cries.

And a crowd gathers 'round an angry young man
Face down in the street with a gun in his hand
In the ghetto.
As her young man dies
On a cold and gray Chicago morning,
Another little baby child is born
In the ghetto
And his mama cries.

It Must Be Him
(Original French Title: "Seul sur son etoile")

Words and Music by Gilbert Becaud and Maurice Vidalin
English Adaptation by Mack David

recorded by Vikki Carr

I tell myself, what's done is done.
I tell myself don't be a fool,
Play the field, have a lot of fun,
It's easy when you play it cool.
I tell myself, don't be a chump,
Who cares? Let him stay away.
That's when the phone rings, and I jump.
And as I grab the phone I pray.

Refrain:
Let it please be him, oh! Dear God,
It must be him. It must be him,
Or I shall die, or I shall die.
Oh! Hello, hello my dear God,
It must be him, but it's not him.
And then I die,
That's when I die.

After a while I'm myself again.
I pick the pieces off the floor,
Put my heart on the shelf again,
He'll never hurt me anymore.
I'm not a puppet on a string,
I'll find somebody new someday,
That's when the phone begins to ring,
And once again I start to pray.

Refrain

Again I die, again I die.

It's Not Unusual

Words and Music by Gordon Mills and Les Reed

recorded by Tom Jones

It's not unusual to be loved by anyone.
It's not unusual to have fun with anyone.
But when I see you hanging about with anyone,
It's not unusual to see me cry. I wanna die.

It's not unusual to go out at anytime,
But when I see you out and about it's such a crime.
If you should ever wanna be loved by anyone,
It's not unusual, it happens every day.
No matter what you say,
You'll find it happens all the time.
Love will never do what you want it to.
Why can't this crazy love be mine?

It's not unusual to be mad with anyone.
It's not unusual to be sad with anyone.
But if I ever find that you've changed at anytime,
It's not unusual to find that I'm in love with you.

King of the Road

Words and Music by Roger Miller

recorded by Roger Miller

Trailer for sale or rent,
Room to let, fifty cents.
No phone, no pool, no pets,
I ain't got no cigarettes.
Ah, but two hours of pushing broom,
Buys an eight by twelve, four bit room.
I'm a man of means by no means,
King of the road.

Third box car midnight train,
Destination Bangor, Maine.
Old worn out suit and shoes,
I don't pay no union dues.
I smoke old stogies I have found,
Short but not big around.
I'm a man of means by no means,
King of the road.

I know every engineer on every train,
All of the children and all of their names,
And every handout in every town,
And every lock that ain't locked when no one's around.

I sing trailer for sale or rent,
Rooms to let, fifty cents.
No phone, no pool, no pets,
I ain't got no cigarettes.
Ah, but two hours of pushing broom,
Buys an eight by twelve four bit room.
I'm a man of means by no means,
King of the road.

It's Now or Never

Words and Music by Aaron Schroeder and Wally Gold

recorded by Elvis Presley

Refrain:
It's now or never
Come hold me tight.
Kiss me, my darlin'
Be mine tonight.
Tomorrow will be too late.
It's now or never,
My love won't wait.

When I first saw you
With your smile so tender,
My heart was captured
My soul surrendered.
I've spent a lifetime
Waiting for the right time.
Now that you're near
The time is here at last.

Refrain

Just like a willow
We could cry an ocean,
If we lost true love
And sweet devotion.
Your lips excite me
Let your arms invite me.
For who knows when
We'll meet again this way.

Refrain

Itsy Bitsy Teenie Weenie Yellow Polkadot Bikini

Words and Music by Paul Vance and Lee Pockriss

recorded by Brian Hyland

She was afraid to come out of the locker,
She was as nervous as she could be;
She was afraid to come out of the locker,
She was afraid that somebody would see.

Spoken: (Two, three, four, tell the people what she wore.)

Sung:
It was an itsy bitsy teenie weenie yellow polkadot bikini,
That she wore for the first time today.
An itsy bitsy teenie weenie yellow polkadot bikini,
So in the locker she wanted to stay.

Spoken: (Two, three, four, stick around, we'll tell you more.)

Sung:
She was afraid to come out in the open,
And so a blanket around her she wore;
She was afraid to come out in the open,
And so she sat bundled up on the shore.

Spoken: (Two, three, four, tell the people what she wore.)

Sung:
It was an itsy bitsy teenie weenie yellow polkadot bikini,
That she wore for the first time today.
An itsy bitsy teenie weenie yellow polkadot bikini,
So in the blanket she wanted to stay.

Spoken: (Two, three, four, stick around, we'll tell you more.)

Sung:
Now she's afraid to come out of the water,
And I wonder what she's gonna do;
Now she's afraid to come out of the water,
And the poor little girl's turning blue.

Spoken: (Two, three, four, tell the people what she wore.)

Sung:
It was an itsy bitsy teenie weenie yellow polkadot bikini,
That she wore for the first time today.
An itsy bitsy teenie weenie yellow polkadot bikini,
So in the water she wanted to stay.

From the locker to the blanket,
From the blanket to the shore,
From the shore to the water,
Guess there isn't any more.

L-O-V-E

Words and Music by Bert Kaempfert and Milt Gabler

recorded by Nat King Cole

L is for the way you look at me.
O is for the only one I see.
V is very, very extraordinary.
E is even more than anyone that you adore can.

Love is all that I can give to you,
Love is more than just a game for two.
Two in love can make it.
Take my heart and please don't break it,
Love was made for me and you.

Repeat Song

(That's almost true) For me and you.

The Little Old Lady (From Pasadena)

Words and Music by Don Altfeld and Roger Christian

recorded by Jan & Dean

The little old lady from Pasadena
(Go Granny, go Granny, go Granny go)
Has a pretty little flower bed of white gardenias.
(Go Granny, go Granny, go Granny go)
But parked in a rickety old garage,
There's a brand new shiny red super-stocked Dodge.

Refrain:
And everybody's sayin' that there's nobody meaner
Than the little old lady from Pasadena.
She drives real fast and she drives real hard.
She's the terror of Colorado Boulevard.
It's the little old lady from Pasadena!

If you see her on the strip don't try to choose her.
(Go Granny, go Granny, go Granny go)
You might have a goer, but you'll never lose her.
(Go Granny, go Granny, go Granny go)
She's gonna get a ticket now, sooner or later,
'Cause she can't keep her foot off the accelerator.

Refrain

You'll see her all the time, just gettin' her kicks now,
(Go Granny, go Granny, go Granny go)
With her four-speed stick and a four-two-six now.
(Go Granny, go Granny, go Granny go)
The guys come to race her from miles around,
But she'll give 'em a length, then she'll shut 'em down.

Refrain

Leaving on a Jet Plane

Words and Music by John Denver

recorded by Peter, Paul & Mary

All my bags are packed, I'm ready to go,
I'm standing here outside your door,
I hate to wake you up to say goodbye.

But the dawn is breakin', it's early morn,
The taxi's waitin', he's blowin' his horn.
Already I'm so lonesome I could cry.

Refrain:
So kiss me and smile for me,
Tell me that you'll wait for me,
Hold me like you'll never let me go.
'Cause I'm leavin' on a jet plane,
Don't know when I'll be back again.
Oh babe, I hate to go.

There's so many times I've let you down;
So many times I've played around,
I tell you now they don't mean a thing.
Every place I go I'll think of you,
Every song I sing I'll sing for you
When I come back I'll bring [wear] your wedding ring.

Refrain

Now the time has come to leave you,
One more time let me kiss you,
Then close your eyes, I'll be on my way.
Dream about the days to come,
When I won't have to leave alone.
About the times I won't have to say:

Refrain

'Cause I'm leavin' on a jet plane,
Don't know when I'll be back again...

Let It Be Me (Je t'appartiens)

English Words by Mann Curtis
French Words by Pierre DeLanoe
Music by Gilbert Becaud

recorded by The Everly Brothers, Betty Everett & Jerry Butler

I bless the day I found you,
I want to stay around you,
And so I beg you,
Let it be me.

Don't take this heaven from one,
If you must cling to someone,
Now and forever,
Let it be me.

Each time we meet, love,
I find complete love,
Without your sweet love,
What would life be?

So never leave me lonely,
Tell me you'll love me only,
And that you'll always
Let it be me.

If, for each bit of gladness,
Someone must taste of sadness,
I'll bear the sorrow,
Let it be me.

No matter what the price is,
I'll make the sacrifices,
Through each tomorrow,
Let it be me.

To you I'm praying,
Hear what I'm saying,
Please let your heart beat
For me, just me.

And never leave me lonely,
Tell me you'll love me only,
And that you'll always
Let it be me.

Let's Hang On

Words and Music by Bob Crewe, Denny Randell and Sandy Linzer

recorded by The Four Seasons

There ain't no good in our goodbyein'.
True love takes a lot of tryin'.
Oh, I'm cryin'.

Refrain:
Let's hang on to what we got.
Don't let go, girl, we got a lot.
Got a lot of love between us.
Hang on, hang on, hang on to what we got.

You say you're gonna go and call it quits,
Gonna chuck it all and break our love to bits.
I wish you never said it.
No, no, we'll both regret it.
That little chip of diamond on your hand
Ain't a fortune, baby,
But you know its stands.

A love to tie and bind us,
We just can't leave behind us.
Baby, baby, baby, stay...

Refrain

There isn't anything I wouldn't do.
I'd pay any price to get in good with you.
Give me a second turnin'.
Don't cool off while I'm burnin'.
You got me cryin', dyin' at your door.
Don't shut me out,
Let me in once more.
Your arms I need to hold to.
Your heart, oh girl, I told you,
Baby, baby, baby, stay.

Refrain

Little Green Apples

Words and Music by Bobby Russell

recorded by O.C. Smith

When I wake up in the morning
With my hair down in my eyes
And she says, "Hi,"
And I stumble to the breakfast table
While the kids are going off to school, goodbye.
And she reaches out and takes my hand,
Squeezes it says, "How you feelin', Hon?"
And I look across at smiling lips
That warm my heart and see the morning sun.
And if that's not lovin' me, then all I've got to say,

Refrain:
God didn't make little green apples,
And it don't rain in Indianapolis in the summertime.
There's no such thing as Doctor Seuss, Disneyland
And Mother Goose is no nursery rhyme.

God didn't make little green apples,
And it don't rain in Indianapolis in the summertime.
And when myself is feelin' low
I think about her face aglow to ease my mind.

Sometimes I call her up at home
Knowing she's busy.
And ask if she could get away
And meet me and grab a bite to eat.
And she drops what she's doin' and
Hurries down to meet me and I'm always late.
But she sits waiting patiently
And smiles when she first sees me
'Cause she's made that way.
And if that's not lovin' me, then all I've got to say,

Refrain

Repeat and Fade:
God didn't make little green apples,
And it don't rain in Indianapolis in the summertime.

Little Sister

Words and Music by Doc Pomus and Mort Shuman

recorded by Elvis Presley

Refrain:
Little sister, don't you, little sister, don't you,
Little sister, don't you kiss me once or twice,
Tell me that it's nice and then you run.
Yeah, yeah, little sister,
Don't you do what your big sister done.

You know I dated your big sister.
Oh, I took her to the show.
Hey, I went for some candy,
Along came Jim Dandy
And they slipped right out the door.

Refrain

I used to pull down on your pigtails,
Hey, girl, pinch your turned up nose.
Aw, but, baby, you've been growin'
And lately it's been showin'
From your head down to your toes.

Refrain

Hey, every time I see your sister,
Lord, she's with somebody new.
Aw, she's mean and she's evil
Like a little old boll weevil,
Think I'll try my luck with you.

Refrain

Well, little sister,
Don't you do what your big sister done.
Ah, little sister,
Don't you do what your big sister done.

The Loco-Motion

Words and Music by Gerry Goffin and Carole King

recorded by Little Eva

Everybody's doin' a brand new dance now.
(C'mon, baby, do the Locomotion.)
I know you'll get to like it if you give it a chance now.
(C'mon, baby, do the Locomotion.)
My little baby sister can do it with ease,
Its easier than learnin' your A-B-C's.
So come on, come on, do the Locomotion with me.
You gotta swing your hips now.
Come on, baby, jump up, jump back.
Oh, well, I think you got the knack.

Now that you can do it, let's make a chain now.
(C'mon, baby, do the Locomotion.)
A chug-a chug-a motion like a railroad train now.
(C'mon, baby, do the Locomotion.)
Do it nice and easy now, don't lose control,
A little bit of rhythm and a lot of soul.
Come on, come on and do the Locomotion with me.
(C'mon, baby, do the Locomotion.)

Move around the floor in a locomotion.
(C'mon, baby, do the Locomotion.)
Do it holdin' hands if you get the notion.
(C'mon, baby, do the Locomotion.)
There's never been a dance that's so easy to do.
It even makes you happy when you're feelin' blue.
So, come on, come on, do the Locomotion with me.
(C'mon, baby, do the Locomotion.)
(C'mon, baby, do the Locomotion.)

Love (Can Make You Happy)

Words and Music by Jack Sigler, Jr.

recorded by Mercy

Wake up in the morning, with the sunshine in your eyes,
And the smell of flowers blooming in the air.
Your mind is filled with the thoughts of a certain someone that you
    love.
And your life is filled with joy when she is there.

Love can make you happy if you find someone who cares
To give a lifetime to you and who has a lot to share.

If you think you've found someone you'll love forevermore,
Then it's worth the price you'll have to pay.
To have to hold's important then forever is the praise.
That means a love you find is goin' to stay.

Love can make you happy if you find someone who cares
To give a lifetime to you and who has a lot to share.

Love, love, love, love, love can make you happy.
Love can make you happy. Love.

The Look of Love

Words by Hal David
Music by Burt Bacharach

from *Casino Royale*
recorded by Sergio Mendes & Brasil '66

The look of love is in your eyes,
A look your smile can't disguise.
The look of love, it's saying so
Much more than just words could ever say
And what my heart has heard,
Well, it takes my breath away.

I can hardly wait to hold you,
Feel my arms around you,
How long I have waited,
Waited just to love you,
Now that I have found you,
Don't ever go.

You've got the look of love
It's on your face,
A look that time can't erase.
Be mine tonight, let this be just
The start of so many nights like this
Let's take a lover's vow
And then seal it with a kiss.

I can hardly wait to hold you,
Feel my arms around you,
How long I have waited,
Waited just to love you,
Now that I have found you
Don't ever go,
Don't ever go,
I love you so.

Monster Mash

Words and Music by Bobby Pickett and Leonard Capizzi

recorded by Bobby "Boris" Pickett

Spoken:
I was working in the lab, late one night,
When my eyes beheld an eerie sight,
For my monster from his slab began to rise,
And suddenly, to my surprise,

Refrain, sung:
He did the mash. (*spoken:* He did the monster mash.)
The monster mash. (*spoken:* It was a graveyard smash.)
He did the mash. (*spoken:* It caught on in a flash.)
He did the mash. (*spoken:* He did the monster mash.)

Spoken:
From my laboratory in the castle east,
To the master bedroom where the vampires feast,
The ghouls all came from their humble abodes
To get a jolt from my electrodes.

Refrain

Spoken:
The zombies were having fun.
The party had just begun.
The guests included Wolfman,
Dracula and his son.

The scene was rockin'. All were digging the sounds.
Igor on chains, backed by his baying hounds.
The coffin-bangers were about to arrive
With their vocal group, "The Crypt-Kicker Five."

Refrain

Spoken:
Out from his coffin, Drac's voice did ring.
Seems he was troubled by just one thing.
He opened the lid and shook his fist,
And said, "Whatever happened to my Transylvanian Twist?"

Refrain

Spoken:
Now everything's cool, Drac's a part of the band.
And my monster mash is the hit of the land.
For you, the living, this mash was meant, too,
When you get to my door, tell them Boris sent you.

Refrain

Spoken:
Mash good. Easy, Igor, you impetuous young boy.

Moon River

Words by Johnny Mercer
Music by Henry Mancini

from the Paramount Picture *Breakfast At Tiffany's*
recorded by Jerry Butler, Henry Mancini

Moon River, wider than a mile;
I'm crossing you in style someday.
Old dream maker, you heart breaker,
Wherever you're goin', I'm goin' your way.

Two drifters, off to see the world.
There's such a lot of world to see.
We're after the same rainbow's end.
Waitin' 'round the bend,
My Huckleberry friend,
Moon River and me.

More (Ti guarderò nel cuore)

Music by Nino Oliviero and Riz Ortolani
Italian Lyrics by Marcello Ciorciolini
English Lyrics by Norman Newell

from the film *Mondo Cane*
recorded by Kai Winding

More than the greatest love the world has known;
This is the love I'll give to you alone.
More than the simple words I try to say;
I only live to love you more each day.

More than you'll ever know,
My arms long to hold you so,
My life will be in your keeping,
Walking, sleeping, laughing, weeping.

Longer than always is a long, long time,
But far beyond forever you'll be mine.
I know I never lived before,
And my heart is very sure,
No one else could love you more.

My Boyfriend's Back

Words and Music by Robert Feldman, Gerald Goldstein and Richard Gottehrer

recorded by The Angels

My boyfriend's back and you're gonna be in trouble.
(Hey, la-di-la, my boyfriend's back.)
When you see him comin', better cut on the double.
(Hey, la-di-la, my boyfriend's back.)
You've been spreading lies that I was untrue.
(Hey, la-di-la, my boyfriend's back.)
So look out now 'cause he's comin' after you.
(Hey, la-di-la, my boyfriend's back.)
And he knows that you've been tryin',
And he knows that you've been lyin'.

He's been gone for such a long time.
(Hey, la-di-la, my boyfriend's back.)
Now he's back and things will be fine.
(Hey, la-di-la, my boyfriend's back.)

You're gonna be sorry you were ever born.
(Hey, la-di-la, my boyfriend's back.)
'Cause he's kinda big and he's awful strong.
(Hey, la-di-la, my boyfriend's back.)
And he knows about your cheatin',
Now you're gonna get a beatin'.

What made you think he'd believe all your lies?
(Ah-oo, ah-oo.)
You're a big man now, but he'll cut you down to size!
(Ah-oo.)
Wait and see!

My boyfriend's back, he's gonna save my reputation.
(Hey, la-di-la, my boyfriend's back.)
If I were you, I'd take a permanent vacation.
(Hey, la-di-la, my boyfriend's back.)
La-di-la, my boyfriend's back!
La-di-la, my boyfriend's back!

My Cherie Amour

Words and Music by Stevie Wonder, Sylvia Moy and Henry Cosby

recorded by Stevie Wonder

La la la la la la,
La la la la la la.

My cherie amour, lovely as a summer day,
My cherie amour, distant as the Milky Way.
My cherie amour, pretty little one that I adore,
You're the only girl my heart beats for;
How I wish that you were mine.

In a cafe or sometimes on a crowded street,
I've been near you, but you never noticed me.
My cherie amour, won't you tell me how could you ignore
That behind that little smile I wore,
How I wish that you were mine.

La la la la la la,
La la la la la la.

Maybe someday you'll see my face among the crowd.
Maybe someday I'll share your little distant cloud.
Oh cherie amour, pretty little one that I adore,
You're the only girl my heart beats for;
How I wish that you were mine.

La la la la la la,
La la la la la la.

My Girl

Words and Music by William "Smokey" Robinson and Ronald White

recorded by The Temptations

I've got sunshine
On a cloudy day;
When it's cold outside,
I've got the month of May.

Refrain:
I guess you say,
What can make me fell this way?
My girl,
Talking 'bout my girl.

I've got so much honey, the bees envy me;
I've got a sweeter song than the birds in the tree.

Refrain

I don't need no money, fortune or fame.
I've got all the riches, baby,
One man can claim.

Refrain

I've got sunshine on a cloudy day
With my girl;
I've even got the month of May
With my girl.
Talking 'bout, talking 'bout, talking 'bout
My girl.
Woo! My girl.
That's all I can talk about is my girl.

My Guy

Words and Music by William "Smokey" Robinson

recorded by Mary Wells

Nothing you could say can tear me away from my guy.
Nothing you could do 'cause I'm stuck like glue to my guy.
I'm sticking to my guy like a stamp to a letter.
Like birds of a feather, we stick together.
I can tell you from the start
I can't be torn apart
From my guy.

Nothing you could do could make me untrue to my guy.
Nothing you could buy could make me tell a lie to my guy.
I gave my guy my word of honor.
To be faithful and I'm gonna.
You best be believing,
I won't be deceiving
My guy.

As a matter of opinion I think he's tops.
My opinion is he's the cream of the crop.
As a matter of taste to be exact,
He's my ideal as a matter of fact.

No muscle-bound man could take my hand from my guy.
No handsome face could ever take the place of my guy.
He may not be a movie star,
But when it comes to being happy, we are.
There's not a man today
Who could take me away
From my guy.

My Love

Words and Music by Tony Hatch

recorded by Petula Clark

My love is warmer than the warmest sunshine,
Softer than a sigh,
My love is deeper than the deepest ocean,
Wider than the sky.
My love is brighter than the brightest star that shines every night above
And there is nothing in this world that can ever change my love.

Something happened to my heart the day that I met you,
Something that I never felt before.
You are always on my mind no matter what I do,
And every day it seems I want you more.

My love is warmer than the warmest sunshine,
Softer than a sigh,
My love is deeper than the deepest ocean,
Wider than the sky.
My love is brighter than the brightest star that shines every night above
And there is nothing in this world that can ever change my love.

Once I thought that love was meant for anyone else but me.
Once I thought you'd never come my way.
Now it only goes to show how wrong we all can be,
For now I have to tell you every day.

My love is warmer than the warmest sunshine,
Softer than a sigh,
My love is deeper than the deepest ocean,
Wider than the sky.
My love is brighter than the brightest star that shines every night above
And there is nothing in this world that can ever change my love.

Na Na Hey Hey
Kiss Him Goodbye

Words and Music by Arthur Frashuer Dale, Paul Roger Leka and Gary Carla

recorded by Steam

Na na na na, na na na na,
Hey hey hey, goodbye.
He'll never love you the way that I love you,
'Cause if he did, no, no, he wouldn't make you cry.

He might be thrilling, baby,
But my love's so doggone willing so kiss him,
Go on and kiss him goodbye.
Na na na na, hey hey hey, goodbye.

Na na na na, na na na na,
Hey hey hey, goodbye.
He's never near you to comfort and cheer you
When all those sad tears are falling, baby, from your eyes.

He might be thrilling baby,
But my love's so doggone willing so kiss him,
Go on and kiss him goodbye.
Na na na na, hey hey hey, goodbye.

Repeat and Fade:
Na na na na, na na na na,
Hey hey hey, goodbye.

Never My Love

Words and Music by Don Addrisi and Dick Addrisi

recorded by The Association

You ask me if there'll come a time
When I grow tired of you.
Never my love, never my love.

You wonder if this heart of mine
Will lose it's desire for you.
Never my love, never my love.

What makes you think love will end
When you know that my whole life depends on you?
Da da da da, da da da da, da da da da da.
Never my love, never my love.

You say you fear I'll change my mind;
I won't require you.
Never my love, never my love.

How can you think love will end
When I've asked you to spend
Your whole life with me?

The Name Game

By Lincoln Chase and Shirley Elliston

recorded by Shirley Ellis

The name game.

Shirley!
Shirley, Shirley, boberley,
Bonana fana foferley,
Fee fi momerley. Shirley!

Lincoln!
Lincoln, Lincoln, bobincoln,
Bonana fana fofincoln,
Fee fi momincoln. Lincoln!

Come on everybody. I say now let's play a game.
I betcha I can make a rhyme out of anybody's name.
The first letter of the name, I treat it like it wasn't there.
But a "B" or an "F," or an "M" will appear.

And then I say "Bo" add a "B" then I say the name,
Then "Bonana, fana" and "fo."
And then I say the name again with an "f" very plain,
Then a "fee fi" and a "mo."
And then I say the name again with an "M" this time.
And there isn't any name that I can't rhyme.

Arnold!
Arnold, Arnold, bobarnold,
Bonana, fana fofarnold,
Fee fi momarmold. Arnold!

But if the first two letters are ever the same,
Drop them both, then say the name.
Like Bob, Bob, drop the "B's." Bo-ob, or Fred.
Fred, drop the "F's." Fo-red, or Mary,
Mary, drop the "M's," Mo-ary.
That's the only rule that is contrary.

Say "Bo" add a "B" now Tony with a "B,"
Now "Bonana, fana" and "fo."
And now you say the name again with an "f" very plain,
Then a "fee fi" and a "mo."
And then you say the name again with an "M" this time.
And there isn't any name that I can't rhyme.

Tony!
Tony, Tony, boboney,
Bonana fana fofoney,
Fee fi momoney. Tony!

Let's do Billy!
Billy, Billy, bogilly, Bonana fana fofilly,
Fee fi momilly. Billy!

Let's do Marsha!
Marsha, Marsha, bobarsha,
Bonana fana fofarsha,
Fee fi moarsha. Marsha!

Little trick with Nick!
Nick, Nick, bobrick,
Bonana fana, fofick,
Fee fi momick. Nick!

The name game.

(You Make Me Feel Like) A Natural Woman

Words and Music by Gerry Goffin, Carole King and Jerry Wexler

recorded by Aretha Franklin

Lookin' out on the morning rain,
I used to feel uninspired.
And when I knew I'd have to face another day,
Lord, it made me feel so tired.
Before the day I met you,
Like was so unkind.
Your love was the key to my peace of mind,

Refrain 1:
'Cause you make me feel,
You make me feel,
You make me feel like a natural woman.
Oh, baby, what you've done to me!
(What you've done to me!)
You make me feel so good inside. (Good inside.)
And I just want to be (Want to be)
Close to you.
You make me feel so alive!

Refrain 2:
You make me feel,
You make me feel,
You make me feel like a natural, natural woman.

Repeat Refrain 2

When my soul was in the lost and found,
You came along to claim it.
I didn't know just what was wrong with me,
'Til your kiss helped me name it.
Now I'm no longer doubtful
Of what I'm living for,
'Cause if I make you happy
I don't need to do more,

Refrain 1 & 2

A natural woman.

Nowhere Man

Words and Music by John Lennon and Paul McCartney

recorded by The Beatles

He's a real nowhere man,
Sitting in his nowhere land,
Making all his nowhere plans for nobody.

Doesn't have a point of view,
Knows not where he's going to,
Isn't he a bit like you and me?

Nowhere man, please listen;
You don't know what you're missing.
Nowhere man,
The world is at your command.

He's as blind as he can be,
Just sees what he wants to see,
Nowhere man can you see me at all?

Nowhere man, don't worry,
Take you're time, don't hurry.
Leave it all
Till somebody else lends you a hand.

Doesn't have a point of view,
Knows not where he's going to.
Isn't he a bit like you and me?

Nowhere man, please listen;
You don't know what you're missing,
Nowhere man,
The world is at your command.

He's a real nowhere man,
Sitting in his nowhere land,
Making all his nowhere plans for nobody,
Making all his nowhere plans for nobody,
Making all his nowhere plans for nobody.

On Broadway

Words and Music by Barry Mann, Cynthia Weil, Mike Stoller and Jerry Leiber

recorded by The Drifters

They say the neon lights are bright
On Broadway;
They say there's always magic in the air;
But when you're walkin' down the street,
And you ain't had enough to eat,
The glitter rubs right off and you're nowhere.

They say the women treat you fine
On Broadway;
But lookin' at them just gives me the blues;
'Cause how ya gonna make some time,
When all you got is one thin dime,
And one thin dime won't even shine your shoes.

They say that I won't last too long
On Broadway;
I'll catch a Greyhound bus for home, they say;
But they're dead wrong, I know they are.
'Cause I can play this here guitar,
And I won't quit till I'm a star on Broadway.

One Fine Day

Words and Music by Gerry Goffin and Carole King

recorded by The Chiffons

One fine day you'll look at me,
And you will know our love was meant to be.
One fine day
You're gonna want me for your girl.

The arms I long for
Will open wide,
And you'll be proud
To have me walking by your side.
One fine day
You're gonna want me for your girl.

Though I know you're the kind of boy
Who only wants to run around.
I'll keep waiting and someday, darling,
You'll come to me when you want to settle down, oh.

One fine day
We'll meet once more,
And then you'll want the love you threw away before.
One fine day,
You're gonna want me for your girl.

One fine day,
Oh, oh,
One fine day,
You're gonna want me for your girl.
Shoo-be-do-be-do-be-do-be-do wah…

Only the Lonely
(Know the Way I Feel)

Words and Music by Roy Orbison and Joe Melson

recorded by Roy Orbison

Only the lonely know the way I feel tonight.
Only the lonely know this feeling ain't right.
There goes my baby, there goes my heart.
They're gone forever, so far apart.
But only the lonely know why I cry.
Only the lonely.

Only the lonely know the heartaches I've been through.
Only the lonely know I cry and cry for you.
Maybe tomorrow a new romance,
No more sorrow, but that's the chance
You got to take if you're lonely, heartbreak.
Only the lonely.

Our Day Will Come

Words by Bob Hilliard
Music by Mort Garson

recorded by Ruby & The Romantics

Our day will come and we'll have everything.
We'll share the joy falling in love can bring.
No one can tell me that I'm too young to know,
I love you so and you love me.

Our day will come if we just wait awhile.
No tears for us, think love and wear a smile.
Our dreams have magic because
We'll always stay in love this way,
Our day will come.

People Got to Be Free

Words and Music by Felix Cavaliere and Edward Brigati, Jr.

recorded by The Rascals

All the world over, it's so easy to see,
People everywhere just wanna be free.
Listen, please listen that's the way it should be.
Peace in the valley, people got to be free.

You should see what a lovely, lovely world this would be.
If everyone learned to live together.
Seems to me, such an easy, easy thing it should be.
Why can't you and me learn to love one another?

All the world over, it's so easy to see,
People everywhere just wanna be free.
Can't understand, it's so simple to me,
People everywhere just got to be free.

If there's man who is down and needs a helping hand,
All it takes is you to understand and to pull him through.
Seems to me, we got to solve it individually,
And I'll do unto you what you do to me.

They'll be shoutin' from the mountain on out to the sea,
No two ways about it, people have to be free.
Ask me my opinion, my opinion will be,
It's a natural situation for man to be free.

Oh what a feelin' just come over me,
It's enough to move a mountain, make a blind man see.
Everybody's dancin', come on let's go see,
There's peace in the valley, now we all can be free.

Spoken:
Look, see that train over there?
Now that's the train of freedom,
It's about to arrive any minute now.
You know it's been long overdue,
Look out 'cause it's comin' right on through.

Poor Side of Town

Words and Music by Johnny Rivers and Lou Adler

recorded by Johnny Rivers

How can you tell me how much you miss me?
When the last time I saw you, you wouldn't even kiss me?
That rich guy you've been seein' must have put you down;
So welcome back baby to the poor side of town.

To him you were nothing but a little plaything.
Not much more than an overnight fling.
To me you were the greatest thing this boy had ever found;
And girl, it's hard to find nice things on the poor side of town.

I can't blame you for tryin',
I'm trying' to make it, too.
I've got one little hang up, baby,
I just can't make it without you.

So tell me: "Are you gonna stay, now?
Will you stand by me all the way now?
With you by my side they can't keep us down;
Together we can make it baby, on the poor side of town."

Puff the Magic Dragon

Words and Music by Lenny Lipton and Peter Yarrow

recorded by Peter, Paul & Mary

Puff, the magic dragon, lived by the sea
And frolicked in the autumn mist in a land called Honahlee.
Little Jackie Paper loved that rascal Puff,
And brought him strings and sealing wax and other fancy stuff.

Refrain:
Oh! Puff, the magic dragon, lived by the sea,
And frolicked in the autumn mist in a land called Honahlee.
Puff, the magic dragon, lived by the sea,
And frolicked in the autumn mist in a land called Honahlee.

Together they would travel on a boat with billowed sail;
Jackie kept a lookout perched on Puff's gigantic tail.
Noble kings and princes would bow whene'er they came,
Pirate ships would lower their flag when Puff roared out his name.

Refrain

A dragon lives forever, but not so little boys,
Painted wings and giant rings make way for other toys.
One grey night it happened, Jackie Paper came no more,
And Puff, that magic dragon, he ceased his fearless roar.

Refrain

His head was bent in sorrow, green scales fell like rain;
Puff no longer went to play along the cherry lane.
Without his life-long friend, Puff could not be brave,
So Puff, that mighty dragon, sadly slipped into his cave.

Refrain

Puppy Love

Words and Music by Paul Anka

recorded by Paul Anka

And they called it puppy love,
Oh, I guess they'll never know,
How a young heart really feels,
And why I love her so.

And they called it puppy love
Just because we're in our teens,
Tell them all it isn't fair
To take away my only dream.

I cry each night my tears for you,
My tears are all in vain.
I'll hope and I'll pray that maybe someday
You'll be back in my arms once again.

Someone help me, help me please,
Is the answer up above?
How can I, how can I tell them
This is not a puppy love.

Raindrops

Words and Music by Dee Clark

recorded by Dee Clark

Raindrops, so many raindrops.
It feels like raindrops
Falling from my eye-eyes,
Falling from my eyes.

Since my love has left me, I'm so all alone,
I would bring her back to me
But I don't know where she's gone,
I don't know where she's gone.

There must be a cloud in my head.
Rain keeps falling from my eye-eyes.
Oh, no, it can't be teardrops,
'Cause a man ain't supposed to cry.

So it must be raindrops, so many raindrops.
It feels like raindrops
Falling from my eye-eyes,
Falling from my eyes.

Reach Out, I'll Be There

Words and Music by Brian Holland, Lamont Dozier and Edward Holland

recorded by The Four Tops

Now, if you feel that you can't go on
Because all of your hope is gone,
And your life is filled with much confusion
Until happiness is just an illusion,
And your world around is crumblin' down;
Darling, reach out, reach out.

I'll be there, with a love that will shelter you.
I'll be there, with a love that will see you through.

When you feel lost and about to give up
'Cause your best just ain't good enough
And you feel the world has grown cold,
And you're drifting out all on your own,
And you need a hand to hold;
Darling, reach out, reach out.

I'll be there, to love and comfort you,
And I'll be there, to cherish and care for you.

I'll be there to always see you through.
I'll be there to love and comfort you.

I can tell the way you hang your head,
You're without love and now you're afraid.
And through your tears you look around,
But there's no peace of mind to be found,
Spoken: I know what you're thinkin'
You're alone now, no love of your own, but
Sung: Darling, reach out, reach out.

I'll be there, to give you all the love you need,
And I'll be there, you can always depend on me.

Release Me

Words and Music by Robert Yount, Eddie Miller and Dub Williams

recorded by Engelbert Humperdinck, Esther Phillips

Please release me, let me go,
For I don't love you anymore.
To waste our lives would be a sin;
Release me and let me love again.

I have found a new love, dear,
And I will always want her near.
Her lips are warm while yours are cold;
Release me, my darling, let me go.

Please release me, can't you see
You'd be a fool to cling to me?
To live a lie would bring us pain,
So release me and let me love again.

Respect

Words and Music by Otis Redding

recorded by Aretha Franklin

What you want, baby I got.
What you need, you know I got it.
All I'm asking is for a little respect, when you come home.
Baby, when you come home, respect.

I ain't gonna do you wrong while you gone.
I ain't gonna do you wrong 'cause I don't wanna.
All I'm asking is for a little respect, when you come home.
Baby, when you come home, respect.

I'm out to give you all my money.
But all I'm askin' in return, honey,
Is to give me my proper respect when you get home.
Yeah, baby, when you get home.

Ooh, your kisses, sweeter than honey.
But guess what, so here's my money.
All I want you to do for me is give me some here,
When you get home. Yeah, baby, when you get home.

R-E-S-P-E-C-T, find out what it means to me,
R-E-S-P-E-C-T, take out T-C-P.

Repeat and Fade:
A little respect.

Return to Sender

Words and Music by Otis Blackwell and Winfield Scott

from *Girls! Girls! Girls!*
recorded by Elvis Presley

I gave a letter to the postman;
He put it in his sack.
Bright and early next morning he brought my letter back.

Refrain:
She wrote up on it:
Return to sender, address unknown.
No such number, no such zone.

We had a quarrel, a lover's spat.
I write to say I'm sorry but my letter keeps coming back.

So then I dropped it in the mailbox
And sent it Special D.
Bright and early next morning, it came right back to me.

Refrain

This time I'm gonna take it myself and put it right in her hand.
And if it comes back the very next day,
Then I'll understand the writing on it.

Twice:
Return to sender, address unknown. No such number, no such zone.

Roses Are Red (My Love)

Words and Music by Al Byron and Paul Evans

recorded by Bobby Vinton

A long, long time ago on graduation day
You handed me your book, I signed this way:
Roses are red, my love, violets are blue,
Sugar is sweet my love, but not as sweet as you.

We dated through high school and when the big day came,
I wrote into your book next to my name:
Roses are red, my love, violets are blue,
Sugar is sweet my love, but not as sweet as you.

Then I went far away and you found someone new.
I read your letter, dear, and I wrote back to you:
Roses are red, my love, violets are blue,
Sugar is sweet my love, good luck, may God bless you.

Is that your little girl? She looks a lot like you.
Someday some boy will write in her book, too:
Roses are red, my love, violets are blue,
Sugar is sweet my love, but not as sweet as you.

Revolution

Words and Music by John Lennon and Paul McCartney

recorded by The Beatles

You say you want a revolution
Well, you know
We all want to change the world
You tell me that it's evolution
Well, you know
We all want to change the world

But when you talk about destruction
Don't you know that you can count me out
Don't you know it's going to be alright
Alright, alright

You say you want a real solution
Well, you know
We'd all love to see the plan
You ask me for a contribution
Well, you know
We're doing what we can

But if you want money for people with minds that hate
All I can tell you is brother you have to wait
Don't you know it's going to be alright
Alright, alright

You say you'll change the Constitution
Well, you know
We all want to change your head
You tell me it's the institution
Well, you know
You better free your mind instead

But if you go carrying pictures of Chairman Mao
You ain't going to make it with me, anyhow
Don't you know it's going to be alright
Alright, alright
Alright, alright…

Ruby Baby

Words and Music by Jerry Leiber and Mike Stoller

recorded by Dion

I love a girl and-a Ruby is her name.
This girl don't love me but I love her just the same.
Ruby, Ruby, how I want ya,
Like a ghost I'm a-gonna haunt ya.
Ruby, Ruby, Ruby, will you be mine?

Each time I see you, baby, my heart cries.
Tell ya, I'm gonna steal you away from all those guys.
From the happy day I met ya,
I made a bet that I was gonna get ya.
Ruby, Ruby, Ruby, will you be mine?

Four Times:
Ruby, Ruby, Ruby, baby.

I love this girl, I said-a Ruby is her name.
When this girl looks at me, she just sets my soul aflame.
Got some huggin' and kisses too, yeah,
And I'm gonna give them-a all to you.
Now listen, Ruby, Ruby, when will you be mine?
Ruby, Ruby, when will you be mine?

Runaway

Words and Music by Del Shannon and Max Crook

recorded by Del Shannon

As I walk along I wonder
What went wrong with our love,
A love that was so strong.
And as I still walk on,
I think of the things we've done together,
While our hearts were young.

I'm a-walkin' in the rain.
Tears are fallin' and I feel a pain,
A-wishin' you were here by me
To end this misery.
And I wonder, wo-wo-wo-wo-wonder
Why, why-why-why-why-why she ran away,
And I wonder where she will stay,
My little runaway, run-run-run-run-runaway.

San Francisco (Be Sure to Wear Some Flowers in Your Hair)

Words and Music by John Phillips

recorded by Scott McKenzie

If you're going to San Francisco,
Be sure to wear some flowers in your hair.
If you're goin' to San Francisco,
You're gonna meet some gentle people there.

For those who come to San Francisco,
Summertime will be a love-in there.
In the streets of San Francisco,
Gentle people with flowers in their hair.

All across the nation, such a strong vibration:
People in motion.
There's a whole generation with a new explanation,
People in motion, people in motion.

For those who come to San Francisco,
Be sure to wear some flowers in your hair.
If you come to San Francisco,
Summertime will be a love-in there.

If you come to San Francisco,
Summertime will be a love-in there.

Sherry

Words and Music by Bob Gaudio

recorded by The Four Seasons

Sherry, Sherry baby,
Sherry, Sherry baby.
Sherry baby, Sherry baby,
Sherry, can you come out tonight?
Come, come, come out tonight.
Sherry baby, Sherry baby,
Sherry, can you come out tonight?

Why don't you come on to my twist party?
Come on where the bright moon shines.
Come on, we'll dance the night away.
I'm gonna make you mine.

Sherry baby, Sherry baby,
Sherry, can you come out tonight?
Come, come, come out tonight.
Come, come, come out tonight.

You better ask your mama, Sherry baby.
Tell her everything is all right.
Why don't you come on, put your red dress on?
Come on, mm, you look so fine.
Come on, move it nice and easy.
Girl, you make me lose my mind.

Sherry baby, Sherry baby,
Sherry, can you come out tonight?
Come, come, come out tonight.
Come, come, come out tonight.
Sherry baby, Sherry baby,
Come, come, come out tonight.

Save the Last Dance for Me

Words and Music by Doc Pomus and Mort Shuman

recorded by The Drifters

You can dance every dance
With the one that gives you the eye;
Let him hold you tight.
You can smile every smile
For the one that holds your hand
In the pale moonlight.

Refrain:
Just don't forget who's taking you home
And in whose arms you're gonna be.
So darlin', save the last dance for me.

Oh, I know that the music is fine,
Like sparkling wine;
Go and have your fun.
Laugh and sing, but while we're apart
Don't give your heart to anyone.

Refrain

Baby, don't you know I love you so?
Can't you feel it when we touch?
I will never, never let you go.
I love you, oh, so much.

You can dance, go and carry on
Till the night is gone,
Till it's time to go.
If he asks if you're all alone,
Can he take you home,
You've got to tell him no.

'Cause don't forget who's taking you home,
And in whose arms you're gonna be.
So darlin', save the last dance for me.

The Shoop Shoop Song (It's in His Kiss)

Words and Music by Rudy Clark

recorded by Betty Everett

Does he love me? I wanna know.
How can I tell if he loves me so?
(Is it in his eyes?) Oh, no, you'll be deceived.
(Is it in his eyes?) Oh, no, you'll make believe.
If you wanna know if he loves you so,
It's in his kiss.

(Is it in his face?) No, no, that's just his charm.
(In his warm embrace?) No, that's just his arm.
If you wanna know if he loves you so,
It's in his kiss.

Refrain:
Hug him and squeeze him tight,
And find out what you wanna know.
If it's love, if it really is,
It's there in his kiss.

(About the way he acts?) Oh, no, that's not the way,
And you're not listenin' to all that I say.
If you wanna know if he loves you so,
It's in his kiss.

Refrain

It's in his kiss. (That's where it is.)
It's in his kiss. (That's where it is.)

Sixteen Reasons
(Why I Love You)

Words and Music by Bill Post and Doree Post

recorded by Connie Stevens

One—the way you hold my hand,
Two—your laughing eyes,
Three—the way you understand,
Four—your secret sighs.
They're all part of sixteen reasons
Why I love you.

Five—the way you comb your hair,
Six—your freckled nose,
Seven—the way you say you care,
Eight—your crazy clothes.
That is just half of the sixteen reasons
Why I love you.

Nine—snuggling in the car,
Ten—your wish upon a star,
Eleven—whispering on the phone.
Twelve—your kiss when we're alone,
Thirteen—the way you thrill my heart,
Fourteen—your voice so neat,
Fifteen—you say we'll never part,
Sixteen—our love's complete.
Those are all of sixteen reasons
Why I love you.

Shop Around

Words and Music by Berry Gordy and William "Smokey" Robinson

recorded by The Miracles

When I became of age,
My mother called me to her side.
She said, "Son, you're growing up now.
Pretty soon you'll take a bride."
And then she said,

Just because you've become a young man now,
There's still some things that you don't understand now.
Before you ask some girl for her hand now,
Keep your freedom for as long as you can now.

My mama told me, you better shop around.
Oh, yeah, you better shop around.

Ah, there's some things that I want you to know now.
Just as sure as the winds gonna blow now,
The women come and the women go now.
Before you tell 'em that you love 'em so now,

My mama told me, you better shop around.
Oh, yeah, you better shop around.

Try to get yourself a bargain, son.
Don't be sold on the very first one.
Pretty girls come a dime a dozen.
A-try to find one who's gonna give you true lovin'.
Before you take a girl and say "I do," now,
Make sure she's in love with you now.
My mama told me, you better shop around.

Try to get yourself a bargain, son.
Don't be sold on the very first one.
Pretty girls come a dime a dozen.
A-try to find one who's gonna give you true lovin'.
Before you take a girl and say "I do," now,
Make sure she's in love with you now.
Make sure that her love is true now.
I hate to see you feelin' sad and blue now.
My mama told me, you better shop around.

Somebody to Love

Words and Music by Darby Slick

recorded by Jefferson Airplane

When the truth is found to be lies,
And all the joy within you dies,
Don't you want somebody to love?
Don't you need somebody to love?
Wouldn't you love somebody to love?
You better find somebody to love.

When the garden's flowers, baby, are dead,
Yes, and your mind, your mind is so full of red,
Don't you want somebody to love?
Don't you need somebody to love?
Wouldn't you love somebody to love?
You better find somebody to love.

Your eyes, I say your eyes may look like his.
Yeah, but in your head, baby, I'm afraid you don't know where it is.
Don't you want somebody to love?
Don't you need somebody to love?
Wouldn't you love somebody to love?
You better find somebody to love.

Tears are running, they're all running down your breast,
And your friends, baby, they treat you like a guest.
Don't you want somebody to love?
Don't you need somebody to love?
Wouldn't you love somebody to love?
You better find somebody to love.

Soul Man

Words and Music by Isaac Hayes and David Porter

recorded by Sam & Dave

Comin' to you on a dusty road,
Good lovin' I got a truckload.
And when you get it you got somethin'.
So don't worry 'cause I'm comin'
I'm a soul man, I'm a soul man,
I'm a soul man. I'm a soul man.

Got what I got the hard way
And I'll make it better each and every day.
So honey, don't you fret,
'Cause you ain't seen nothin' yet.
I'm a soul man, I'm a soul man,
I'm a soul man. I'm a soul man.

I was brought up on a side street.
I learned how to love before I could eat.
I was educated at Woodstock.
When I start lovin' I just can't stop.
I'm a soul man, I'm a soul man,
I'm a soul man. I'm a soul man.

Well, grab your rope and I'll push you in,
Give you hope and be your only boyfriend.
I'm a soul man, I'm a soul man,
I'm a soul man. I'm a soul man.

Someday We'll Be Together

Words and Music by Jackey Beavers, Johnny Bristol and Harvey Fuqua

recorded by Diana Ross & The Supremes

Mm mm.
Mm mm mm mm.

Someday we'll be together.
Say it, say it, say it, say it again. You tell 'em.
Someday we'll be together.
Oh yeah, oh yeah.

You're far away from me, my love.
And just as sure, my, my baby,
As there are stars above.
I wanna say, I wanna say, I wanna say it.

Someday we'll be together.
Yes, we will. Yes, we will.
Say someday we'll be together.
I know, I know, I know, I know.

My love is yours, baby, oh, right from the start.
You, you, you possess my soul now, honey,
And I know, I know you own my heart.
And I wanna say it.

Someday we'll be together.
Yes, we will. Yes, we will.
Say someday we'll be together.
Yes, we will, yes, we will.

Long time ago, my, my sweet thing,
I made a big mistake, honey.
I say I said goodbye. Oh, oh, baby.
Ever, ever and ever and ever and ever
Ever since that day, now all I,
All I wanna do oh is cry, cry, oh. Hey, hey, hey.

I long for you every, every night.
Just to kiss your sweet lips, baby.
Hold you ever, ever so tight.
And I wanna say it.

Repeat and Fade:
Someday we'll be together.
Ah, yes, we will, yes, we will.

Stand by Me

Words and Music by Jerry Leiber, Mike Stoller and Ben E. King

recorded by Ben E. King

When the night has come and the land is dark
And the moon is the only light we'll see.
No I won't be afraid, no I won't be afraid
Just as long as you stand,
Stand by me.

Refrain:
So darling, darling,
Stand by me,
Oh, stand by me,
Oh, stand,
Stand by me,
Stand by me.

If the sea that we look upon should tumble and fall
Or the mountain crumble in the sea.
I won't cry, no I won't shed a tear
Just as long as you stand,
Stand by me.

Refrain

Whenever you're in trouble won't you stand by me
Oh, stand by me,
Oh, stand by me,
Stand by me.

Refrain

Stay

Words and Music by Maurice Williams

recorded by Maurice Williams & The Zodiacs, The Four Seasons

Dance just a little bit longer.
Please, please, please, please
Tell me that you're goin' to.
Now, your daddy don't mind
And your mommy don't mind.
Could we have another dance, dear,
Just a one more, one more time?

Oh, won't you stay
Just a little bit longer?
Please let me dance
Please say that you will.

Stop! In the Name of Love

Words and Music by Lamont Dozier, Brian Holland and Edward Holland

recorded by The Supremes

Stop! In the name of love
Before you break my heart.
Baby, baby, I'm aware of where you go
Each time you leave my door.
I watch you walk down the street,
Knowing your other love you meet.
But this time before you run to her
Leaving me alone to cry:

Haven't I been good to you?
Haven't I been sweet to you?
Stop! In the name of love
Before you break my heart,
Stop! In the name of love
Before you break my heart.
Think it over,
Think it over.

I've known of your,
Your secluded nights,
I've even seen her maybe once or twice.
But is her sweet expression
Worth more than my love and affection?
This time before you leave my arms
And rush off to her charms:

Haven't I been good to you?
Haven't I been sweet to you?
Stop! In the name of love
Before you break my heart,
Stop! In the name of love
Before you break my heart.
Think it over,
Think it over.

I've tried so hard,
Hard to be patient
Hoping that you'd stop this infatuation.
But each time you are together
I'm so afraid I'm losing you forever.

Stop! In the name of love
Before you break my heart,
Stop! In the name of love
Before you break my heart.

Strangers in the Night

Words by Charles Singleton and Eddie Snyder
Music by Bert Kaempfert

adapted from *A Man Could Get Killed*
recorded by Frank Sinatra

Strangers in the night exchanging glances,
Wondering in the night what were the chances
We'd be sharing love before the night was though.

Something in your eyes was so inviting,
Something in your smile was so exciting,
Something in my heart told me I must have you.

Strangers in the night, two lonely people,
We were strangers in the night
Up to the moment when we said our first hello
Little did we know love was just a glance away,
A warm embracing dance away.

And ever since that night we've been together,
Lovers at first sight in love forever.
It turned out so right for strangers in the night.

Sunshine of Your Love

Words and Music by Jack Bruce, Pete Brown and Eric Clapton

recorded by Cream

It's getting near dawn when lights close their tired eyes.
I'll soon be with you, my love,
To give you my dawn surprise,
I'll be with you darling, soon.
I'll be with you when the stars start falling.

I've been waiting so long to be where I'm going
In the sunshine of your love.

I'm with you my love; the light shining through on you.
Yes, I'm with you, my love.
It's the morning and just we two.
I'll stay with you darling, now,
I'll stay with you till my seeds are dried up.

I've been waiting so long,
I've been waiting so long,
I've been waiting so long to be where I'm going
In the sunshine of your love.

Surfin' U.S.A.

Words and Music by Chuck Berry

recorded by The Beach Boys

If everybody had an ocean across the U.S.A.
Then everybody'd be surfin', like California.
You'd see them wearin' their baggies
Huarachi sandals too.
A bushy, bushy blond hairdo,
Surfin' U.S.A.

You'll catch 'em surfin' at Del Mar, Ventura County Line,
Santa Cruz and Tressels, Australia's Narabine,
All over Manhattan and down Doheny way.
Everybody's gone surfin', surfin' U.S.A.

Will all be plannin' out a route
We're gonna take real soon,
We're waxing down our surf boards,
We can't wait for June.
We'll all be gone for the summer,
We're on safari to stay.
Tell the teacher we're surfin',
Surfin' U.S.A.

At Haggarty's and Swami's, Pacific Palisades,
San Onofre and Sunset Redondo Beach, L.A.
All over La Jolla, and at Waiamea Bay.
Everybody's gone surfin',
Surfin' U.S.A.

Suspicious Minds

Words and Music by Francis Zambon

recorded by Elvis Presley

We're caught in a trap. I can't walk out,
Because I love you too much, baby.
Why can't you see what you're doing to me
When you don't believe a word I say?
We can't go on together with suspicious minds,
And we can't build our dreams on suspicious minds.

So if an old friend I know stops by to say hello,
Would I still see suspicion in your eyes?
But here we go again, asking where I've been.
You can't see the tears are real I'm crying.
We can't go on together with suspicious minds,
And we can't build our dreams on suspicious minds.

Oh, let our love survive,
Or drive the tears from your eyes.
Let's don't let a good thing die, when, honey,
You know I've never lied to you. Mm, yeah, yeah.

We're caught in a trap. I can't walk out,
Because I love you too much, baby.
Why can't you see what you're doing to me
When you don't believe a word I say?
Well, don't you know I'm caught in a trap.
I can't walk out, because I love you too much, baby.

Suspicion

Words and Music by Doc Pomus and Mort Shuman

recorded by Terry Stafford

Every time you kiss me,
I'm still not certain that you love me.
Every time you hold me,
I'm still not certain that you care.
Though you keep on saying
You really, really, really love me,
Do you speak the same words
To someone else when I'm not there?

Refrain:
Suspicion torments my heart.
Suspicion keeps us apart.
Suspicion, why torture me!

Everytime you call me
And tell me we should meet tomorrow,
I can't help but think that
You're meeting someone else tonight.
Why should our romance just
A-keep on causing me such sorrow?
Why am I so doubtful
Whenever you're out of sight?

Refrain

Darling, if you love me,
I beg you, wait a little longer.
Wait until I drive all
These foolish fears out of my mind.
How I hope and pray that
Our love will keep on growing stronger.
Maybe I'm suspicious
'Cause true love is so hard to find.

Refrain

Take Good Care of My Baby

Words and Music by Gerry Goffin and Carole King

recorded by Bobby Vee

My tears are fallin'
'Cause you're takin' her away,
And though it really hurts me so,
There's somethin' that I gotta say.

Take good care of my baby,
Please don't ever make her blue.
Just tell her that you love her,
Make sure you're thinkin' of her
In everything you say and do.
Take good care of my baby,
Don't you ever make her cry.
Just let your love surround her,
Paint a rainbow all around her.
Don't let her see a cloudy sky.

Once upon a time that little girl was mine.
If I'd been true, I know she'd never be with you.
So take good care of my baby,
Be just as kind as you can be.
And if you discover
That you really don't love her,
Just send my baby back home to me.

Teen Angel

Words and Music by Jean Surrey

recorded by Mark Dinning

That fateful night the car was stalled
Upon the railroad track.
I pulled you out and we were safe,
But you went running back.

Refrain:
Teen angel, can you hear me?
Teen angel, can you see me?
Are you somewhere up above,
And am I still your own true love?

What was it you were looking for
That took your life that night?
They said they found my high school ring
Clutched in your fingers tight.

Refrain

Just sweet sixteen, and now you're gone;
They've taken you away.
I'll never kiss your lips again;
They buried you today.

Refrain

Teen angel, teen angel, answer me, please.

Tell It Like It Is

Words and Music by George Davis and Lee Diamond

recorded by Aaron Neville

If you want something to play with
Go and find yourself a toy.
Baby, my time is too expensive,
And I'm not a little boy.
If you are serious, don't play with my heart.
It makes me furious.
But if you want me to love you,
Baby, I will. Girl, you know I will.

Tell it like it is. Don't be ashamed.
Let your conscience be your guide.
But I know deep down inside of me;
I believe you love me. Forget your foolish pride.
Life is too short to have sorrow.
You may be here today and gone tomorrow.
You might as well get what you want,
So go on and live, baby, go on and live.

That's Life

Words and Music by Dean Kay and Kelly Gordon

recorded by Frank Sinatra

That's life, that's what people say.
You're ridin' high in April, shot down in May;
But I know I'm gonna change that tune
When I'm back on top in June.

That's life, funny as it seems,
Some people get their kicks steppin' on dreams;
But I don't let it get me down,
'Cause this ol' world keeps going around.

I've been a puppet, a pauper, a pirate a poet, a pawn and a king.
I've been up and down and over and out and I know one thing;
Each time I find myself flat on my face,
I pick myself up and get back in the race.

That's life, I can't deny it.
I thought of quitting, but my heart just won't buy it.
If I didn't think it was worth a try,
I'd roll myself up in a big ball and die.

There's a Kind of Hush
(All Over the World)

Words and Music by Les Reed and Geoff Stephens

recorded by Herman's Hermits

There's a kind of hush,
All over the world tonight,
All over the world,
You can hear the sounds
Of lovers in love.
You know what I mean.
Just the two of us
And nobody else in sight,
There's nobody else
And I'm feeling good,
Just holding you tight.

So listen very carefully.
Closer now and you will see what I mean.
It isn't a dream.
The only sound that you will hear
Is when I whisper in your ear,
I love you,
Forever and ever.

There's a kind of hush,
All over the world tonight.
All over the world,
You can hear the sounds
Of lovers in love.

Things

Words and Music by Bobby Darin

recorded by Bobby Darin

Every night I sit here by my window (window),
Staring at the lonely avenue (avenue),
Watching lovers holding hands and laughing (laughing),
And thinkin' 'bout the things we used to do.

Refrain:
(Thinkin' of things) Like a walk in the park,
(Things) Like a kiss in the dark,
(Things) Like a sailboat ride,
(Yeah, yeah) What about the night we cried?
Things like a lover's vow,
Things that we don't do now,
Thinkin' 'bout the things we used to do.

Memories are all I have to cling to (cling to),
And heartaches are the friends I'm talking to (talking to).
When I'm not thinkin' of a-just how much I love you (love you),
Well, I'm thinkin' 'bout the things we used to do.

Refrain

I still can hear the jukebox softly playing (playing),
And the face I see each day belongs to you (belongs to you).
Though there's not a single sound and there's nobody else around,
Well, there's a-just me thinkin' 'bout the things we used to do.

Refrain

And the heartaches are the friends I'm talking to.
You got me thinkin' 'bout the things we used to do.
Starin' at the lonely avenue.

This Guy's in Love with You

Lyric by Hal David
Music by Burt Bacharach

recorded by Herb Alpert, Dionne Warwick

You see this guy,
This guy's in love with you.
Yes, I'm in love.
Who looks at you the way I do?
When you smile,
I can tell we know each other very well.
How can I show you
I'm glad I got to know you.
'Cause

I've heard some talk.
They say you think I'm fine.
This guy's in love,
And what I'd do to make you mine.
The me now, is it so?
Don't let me be the last to know.
My hands are shaking.
Don't let my heart keep breaking
'Cause

I need your love,
I want your love.
Say you're in love,
In love with this guy.
If not, I'll just die.

Travelin' Man

Words and Music by Jerry Fuller

recorded by Ricky Nelson

I'm a travelin' man,
And I've made a lot o' stops all over the world.
And in every port I own the heart
Of at least one lovely girl.

I've a pretty señorita waiting for me
Down in old Mexico.
If you're ever in Alaska, stop and see
My cute little Eskimo.

Oh my sweet fraulein down in Berlin town
Makes my heart start to yearn.
And my China doll down in old Hong Kong
Waits for my return.

Pretty Polynesian baby over the sea,
I remember the night
When we walked in the sands of Waikiki
And I held you, oh, so tight.

Repeat All

Oh, I'm a travelin' man. Yes, I'm a travelin' man.

This Land Is Your Land

Words and Music by Woody Guthrie

recorded by Woody Guthrie

This land is your land, this land is my land,
From California to the New York island,
From the redwood forest to the Gulf Stream waters;
This land was made for you and me.

As I was walking that ribbon of highway,
I saw above me the endless skyway;
I saw below me that golden valley;
This land was made for you and me.

I've roamed and rambled and I followed my footsteps,
To the sparkling sand of diamond desserts;
And all around me a voice was sounding;
This land was made for you and me.

When the sun came shining, and I was strolling,
And the wheat fields waving and the dust clouds rolling,
As the fog was lifting a voice was chanting:
This land was made for you and me.

As I went walking, I saw a sign there,
And on the sign it said "No trespassing."
But on the other side it didn't say nothing,
That side was made for you and me.

In the shadow of the steeple, I saw my people,
By the relief office I seen my people;
As they stood there hungry, I stood there asking,
Is this land made for you and me?

Nobody living can ever stop me,
As I go walking that freedom highway;
Nobody living can ever make me turn back.
This land was made for you and me.

Those Were the Days

Words and Music by Gene Raskin

recorded by Mary Hopkin

Once upon a time there was a tavern
Where we used to raise a glass or two.
Remember how we laughed away the hours,
And dreamed of all the great things we would do.

Refrain:
Those were the days my friend.
We thought they'd never end,
We'd sing and dance
Forever and a day;
We'd live the life we choose,
We'd fight and never lose,
For we were young and sure to have our way.
La la la la, la la
La la la la, la la
Those were the days,
Oh yes, those were the days.

Then the busy years went rushing by us.
We lost our starry notions on the way.
If by chance I'd see you in the tavern,
We'd smile at one another and we'd say—

Refrain

Just tonight I stood before the tavern.
Nothing seemed the way it used to be.
In the glass I saw a strange reflection,
Was that lonely fellow really me?

Refrain

Through the door there came familiar laughter.
I saw your face and heard you call my name.
Oh my friends we're older but no wiser,
For in our hearts the dreams are still the same.

Refrain

Turn! Turn! Turn! (To Everything There Is a Season)

Words from the Book of Ecclesiastes
Adaptation and Music by Pete Seeger

recorded by The Byrds

To everything (turn, turn, turn)
There is a season (turn, turn, turn)
And a time for every purpose under heaven.
A time to be born, a time to die
A time to plant, a time to reap;
A time to kill, a time to heal;
A time to laugh, a time to weep.

Refrain:
To everything (turn, turn, turn)
There is a season (turn, turn, turn)
And a time for every purpose under heaven.

A time to build up,
A time to break down;
A time to dance, a time to mourn;
A time to cast away stones,
A time to gather stones together.

Refrain

A time of love, a time of hate;
A time of war, a time of peace;
A time you may embrace,
A time to refrain from embracing.

Refrain

The Twist

Words and Music by Hank Ballard

recorded by Chubby Checker

Come on, baby, let's do the twist.
Come on, baby, let's do the twist.
Take me by my little hand and go like this:

Refrain:
Ee oh twist, baby, baby twist.
('Round and around and around and around)
Just, just like this
('Round and around)
Come on, little miss, and do the twist.
('Round and around)

While Daddy is sleepin' and Mamma ain't around,
While Daddy is sleepin' and Mamma ain't around,
We're gonna twisty, twisty, twisty
Until we tear the house down.

Refrain

You should see my little sis.
You should see my little sis.
She knows how to rock,
And she knows how to twist.

Refrain

Twist and Shout

Words and Music by Bert Russell and Phil Medley

recorded by The Beatles, The Isley Brothers

Refrain:
Well, shake it up, baby, now (shake it up, baby).
Twist and shout (twist and shout).
Come on, come on, come on, come on, baby, now (come on baby).
Come on and work it on out (work it on out).

Well, work it on out (work it on out).
You know you look so good (look so good).
You know you got me goin' now (got me goin'),
Just like I knew you would (like I knew you would).

Refrain

You know you twist, little girl (twist, little girl).
You know you twist so fine (twist so fine).
Come on and twist a little closer now (twist a little closer)
And let me know that you're mine (let me know you're mine).

Ah, ah, ah, ah, ah.

Refrain

You know you twist, little girl (twist, little girl).
You know you twist so fine (twist so fine).
Come on and twist a little closer now (twist a little closer)
And let me know that you're mine (let me know you're mine).

Three Times:
Well, shake it, shake it, shake it, baby, now (shake it up baby).

Ah, ah, ah.

Unchain My Heart

Words and Music by Bobby Sharp and Teddy Powell

recorded by Ray Charles

Unchain my heart. Baby, let me be.
Unchain my heart, 'cause you don't care about me.
You got me sewn up like a pillowcase,
But you let my love go to waste.
So unchain my heart, oh please, please, set me free.

Unchain my heart. Baby, let me go.
Unchain my heart, 'cause you don't love me no more.
Every time I call you on the phone,
Some fella tells me that you're not at home.
So unchain my heart, oh please, please, set me free.

I'm under your spell, like a man in a trance.
But I know darn well that I don't stand a chance.
So unchain my heart. Let me go my way.
Unchain my heart. You worry me night and day.

Why lead me through a life of misery,
When you don't care a bag of beans for me?
So unchain my heart, oh please, please, set me free.

Repeat and Fade:
Oh, won't you set me free?

Up, Up and Away

Words and Music by Jimmy Webb

recorded by The Fifth Dimension

Would you like to ride in my beautiful balloon?
Would you like to glide in my beautiful balloon?
We could float among the stars together, you and I,
For we can fly! (We can fly!)
Up, up and away, my beautiful, my beautiful balloon!

The world's a nicer place in my beautiful balloon.
It wears a nicer face in my beautiful balloon.
We can sing a song and sail along the silver sky,
For we can fly! (We can fly!)
Up, up and away, my beautiful, my beautiful balloon!

Suspended under a twilight canopy,
We'll search the clouds for a star to guide us.
If by some chance you find yourself loving me,
We'll find a cloud to hide us, keep the moon beside us.

Love is waiting there in my beautiful balloon,
Way up in the air in my beautiful balloon.
If you'll hold my hand, we'll chase your dream across the sky,
For we can fly! (We can fly!)
Up, up and away, my beautiful, my beautiful balloon!

Walk Like a Man

Words and Music by Bob Crewe and Bob Gaudio

recorded by The Four Seasons

Oh, how you tried to cut me down to size,
Tellin' dirty lies to my friends.
My own father said, "Give her up, don't bother,
The world isn't coming to an end."

He said, "Walk like a man, talk like a man,
Walk like a man, my son.
No woman's worth crawlin' on the earth,
So walk like a man, my son."

Bye-aye, baby, don't mean maybe;
Gonna get along somehow.
Soon you'll be cryin', account of all your lyin',
Oh yeah, just look who's laughing now.

I'm gonna walk like a man, fast as I can,
Walk like a man from you.
I'll tell the world, forget about it, girl,
And walk like a man from you.

Walk Right In

Words and Music by Gus Cannon and H. Woods

recorded by The Rooftop Singers

Walk right in,
Set right down,
Daddy, let your mind roll on.
Walk right in,
Set right down,
Daddy, let your mind roll on.

Refrain:
Everybody's talkin' 'bout a new way o' walkin',
Do you wanna lose your mind?

Walk right in,
Set right down,
Daddy, let your mind roll on.

Walk right in,
Set right down,
Baby, let your hair hang down.
Walk right in,
Set right down,
Baby, let your hair hang down.

Refrain

Walk right in,
Set right down,
Baby, let your hair hang down.

What the World Needs Now Is Love

Lyric by Hal David
Music by Burt Bacharach

recorded by Jackie DeShannon

Refrain:
What the world needs now is love, sweet love,
It's the only thing that there's just too little of.
What the world needs now is love, sweet love,
No, not just for some, but for everyone.

Lord, we don't need another mountain,
There are mountains and hillsides enough to climb;
There are oceans and rivers enough to cross,
Enough to last, till the end of time.

Refrain

Lord, we don't need another meadow,
There are cornfields and wheat fields enough to grow;
There are sunbeams and moonbeams enough to shine,
Oh, listen, Lord, if you want to know.

Refrain

No not just for some, Oh, but just for everyone.

When I Grow Up
(To Be a Man)

Words and Music by Brian Wilson and Mike Love

recorded by The Beach Boys

When I grow up to be a man,
Will I dig the same things that turn me on as a kid?
Will I look back and say that I wish I hadn't done what I did?
Will I joke around and still dig those sounds
When I grow up to be a man?

Will I look for the same things in a woman that I dig in a girl?
Will I settle down fast or will I first wanna travel the world?
Now I'm young and free, but how will it be
When I grow up to be a man?

Will my kids be proud or think their old me is really a square?
When they're out havin' fun, yeah, will I still wanna have my share?
Will I love my wife for the rest of my life
When I grow up to be a man?

What will I be
When I grow up to be a man?
Won't last forever.
Won't last forever.

Wild Thing

Words and Music by Chip Taylor

recorded by The Troggs

Refrain:
Wild thing, you make my heart sing.
You make everything groovy.
Wild thing.

Spoken: Wild thing, I think I love you.
Sung: But I wanna know for sure.
Spoken: Come on and hold me tight.
I love you.

Refrain

Spoken: Wild thing, I think you move me.
Sung: But I wanna know for sure.
Spoken: Come on and hold me tight.
You move me.

Refrain Twice

Where Did Our Love Go

Words and Music by Brian Holland, Lamont Dozier and Edward Holland

recorded by The Supremes

Baby, baby, baby, don't leave me.
Ooh, please don't leave me all by myself.
I've got this burning, burning, yearning feelin' inside me.
Ooh, deep inside me and it hurts so bad.

You came into my heart (baby, baby) so tenderly,
With a burning love (baby, baby)
That stings like a bee (baby, baby)
Now that I surrender (baby, baby) so helplessly,
You now want to leave (baby, baby)
Ooh, you wanna leave me (baby, baby)
Ooh (baby, baby).

Baby, baby, where did our love go?
Ooh, don't you want me?
Don't you want me no more (baby, baby)?
Ooh, baby.

Baby, baby, where did our love go?
And all your promises of a love forevermore!
I've got this burning, burning, yearning feelin' inside me.
Ooh, deep inside me, and it hurts so bad.

Before you won my heart (baby, baby)
You were a perfect guy.
But now that you got me,
You wanna leave me behind (baby, baby).
Ooh, baby.

Baby, baby, baby don't leave me.
Ooh, please don't leave me all by myself (baby, baby).
Ooh.

Where Have All the Flowers Gone?

Words and Music by Pete Seeger

recorded by The Kingston Trio

Where have all the flowers gone?
Long time passing.
Where have all the flowers gone?
Long time ago.
Where have all the flowers gone?
The girls picked them every one .

Refrain:
Oh, when will they ever learn?
Oh, when will they ever learn?

Where have all the young girls gone?
Long time passing.
Where have all the young girls gone?
They've taken husbands every one.

Refrain

Where have all the young men gone?
Long time passing.
Where have all the young men gone?
Long time ago.
Where have all the young men gone?
They're all in uniform.

Refrain

Where have all the soldiers gone?
Long time passing.
Where have all the soldiers gone?
Long time ago.
Where have all the soldiers gone?
They're gone to graveyards, every one.

Refrain

Where have all the graveyards gone?
Long time passing.
Where have all the graveyards gone?
Long time ago.
Where have all the graveyards gone?
They're covered with flowers, every one.

Refrain

Repeat Verse 1 and Refrain

A Whiter Shade of Pale

Words and Music by Keith Reid and Gary Brooker

recorded by Procol Harum

We skipped the light fandago,
Turned cartwheels 'cross the floor;
I was feeling kind of seasick,
The crowd called out for more.
The room was humming harder
As the ceiling flew away.
When we called for another drink
The waiter brought a tray.

Refrain:
And so it was that later
As the miller told his tale,
That her face, at first just ghostly,
Turned a whiter shade of pale.

She said, "I'm home on shore leave,"
Through in truth we were at sea;
So I took her by the looking glass
And forced her to agree.
Saying, "You must be the mermaid
Who took Neptune for a ride,"
But she smiled at me so sadly
That my anger straightaway died.

Refrain

She said, "There is no reason,
And the truth is plain to see,"
But I wandered through my playing cards
And would not let her be
One of sixteen vestal virgins
Who were leaving for the coast.
And although my eyes were open
They might just as well been closed.

Refrain

Will You Love Me Tomorrow (Will You Still Love Me Tomorrow)

Words and Music by Gerry Goffin and Carole King

recorded by The Shirelles

Tonight you're mine completely.
You give your love so sweetly.
Tonight the light of love is in your eyes,
But will you love me tomorrow?

Is this a lasting treasure
Or just a moment's pleasure?
Can I believe the magic of your sighs?
Will you still love me tomorrow?

Tonight with words unspoken,
You say that I'm the only one.
But will my heart be broken
When the night meets the morning sun?

I'd like to know that your love
Is love that I can be sure of.
So tell me now, and I won't ask again.
Will you still love me tomorrow?
Will you still love me tomorrow?

Wouldn't It Be Nice

Words and Music by Brian Wilson, Tony Asher and Mike Love

recorded by The Beach Boys

Wouldn't it be nice if we were older,
Then we wouldn't have to wait so long.
And wouldn't it be nice to live together
In the kind of world where we'd belong.
Though it's gonna make it that much better
When we can say goodnight and stay together.

Wouldn't it be nice if we could wake up
In the morning when the day is new,
And after that to spend the day together,
Hold each other close the whole night through.
The happy times together we'd been spending,
I wish that every kiss was never ending.
Oh, wouldn't it be nice.

Well, maybe if we think and wish
And hope and pray, it might come true.
Baby, then there wouldn't be
A single thing we couldn't do.
We could be married, and then we'd be happy.
Oh, wouldn't it be nice.

Yester-Me, Yester-You, Yesterday

Words by Ron Miller
Music by Bryan Wells

recorded by Stevie Wonder

What happened to the world we knew,
When we would dream and scheme
And while the time away,
Yester-me, yester-you, yesterday.

Where did it go, that yester-glow,
When we could feel the wheel
Of life turn our way,
Yester-me, yester-you, yesterday.

I had a dream, so did you.
Life was warm, love as true.
Two kids who followed all the rules, yester-fools.
And now, now it seems those yester-dreams
Were just a cruel and foolish game we used to play,
Yester-me, yester-you, yesterday.

When I recall what we had,
I feel lost, I feel sad,
With nothing but the memory of yester-love,
And now, now it seems those yester-dreams
Were just a cruel and foolish game we had to play,
Yester-me, yester-you, yesterday.

Yesterday

Words and Music by John Lennon and Paul McCartney

recorded by The Beatles

Yesterday, all my troubles seemed so far away,
Now it looks as though they're here to stay,
Oh, I believe in yesterday.

Suddenly, I'm not half the man I used to be,
There's a shadow hanging over me,
Oh, yesterday came suddenly.

Bridge:
Why she had to go
I don't know, she wouldn't say.
I said something wrong,
Now I long for yesterday.

Yesterday, love was such an easy game to play.
Now I need a place to hide away,
Oh, I believe in yesterday.

Repeat from Bridge

You've Lost
That Lovin' Feeling

Words and Music by Barry Mann, Cynthia Weil and Phil Spector

recorded by The Righteous Brothers

You never close your eyes anymore when I kiss your lips.
And there's no tenderness like before in your fingertips.
You're trying hard not to show it baby,
But baby, baby I know it.

Refrain:
You've lost that lovin' feeling,
Whoa that lovin' feeling.
You've lost that lovin' feeling.
Now it's gone, gone, gone, whoa.

Now there's no welcome look in your eyes when I reach for you.
And now you're starting to criticize little things I do.
It make me just feel like cryin' baby
'Cause baby, something beautiful's dying.

Refrain

Baby, baby, I'd get down on my knees and pray to you,
If you would only love me like you used to do.
We had a love, a love, a love you don't find ev'ry day.
So don't, don't, don't, don't let it slip away.

Bring back that lovin' feeling,
Whoa that lovin' feeling.
Bring back that lovin' feeling.
Now it's gone, gone, gone,
And I can't go on, whoa.

You've lost that lovin' feeling,
Whoa that lovin' feeling.
You've lost that lovin' feeling.
Now it's gone, gone, gone.

You've Made Me So Very Happy

Words and Music by Berry Gordy, Frank E. Wilson and Patrice Holloway

recorded by Blood, Sweat & Tears

I lost at love before,
Got mad and closed the door.
But you said try just once more.
I chose you for the one,
Now I'm having so much fun.
You treated me so kind,
I'm about to lose my mind.
You made me so very happy,
I'm so glad you came into my life.

The others were untrue,
But when it came to lovin' you,
I'd spend my whole life with you.
'Cause you came and you took control,
You touched my very soul.
You always showed me that
Loving you was where it's at.
You made me so very happy,
I'm so glad you came into my life.

I love you so much, it seems
That you're even in my dream.
I hear you calling me.
I'm so in love with you,
All I ever want to do is
Thank you, baby.

You made me so very happy,
I'm so glad you came into my life.
You made me so very happy,
I'm so glad you came into my life.

You Didn't Have To Be So Nice

Words and Music by John Sebastian and Steve Boone

recorded by The Lovin' Spoonful

You didn't have to be so nice.
I would have liked you anyway,
If you had just looked once or twice
And gone upon your quiet way.
Today said the time was right for me to follow you.
I know I'd find you in a day or two and it's true.
You came upon a quiet day,
You simply seemed to take you place.
I knew that it would be that way
The minute that I saw your face.

And when we've had a few more days,
I wonder if I'll get to say,
"You didn't have to be so nice,
I would've liked you anyway."
Today said the time was right for me to follow you.
I knew I'd find you in a day or two and it's true.
You didn't have to be so nice.
I would have liked you anyway,
If you had just looked once or twice
And gone upon your quiet way.

THE PAPERBACK SONGS SERIES

$7.95 EACH

THE '20s
00240236

THE '30s
00240238

THE '40s
00240239

THE '50s
00240240

THE '60s
00240241

THE '70s
00240242

THE '80s
00240243

THE '90s
00240244

'80s & '90s ROCK
00240126

THE BEACH BOYS
00240261

THE BEATLES
00702008

BIG BAND SWING
00240171

THE BLUES
00702014

BROADWAY SONGS
00240157

CHILDREN'S SONGS
00240149

CHORDS FOR KEYBOARD & GUITAR
00702009

CHRISTMAS CAROLS
00240142

CHRISTMAS SONGS
00240208

CLASSIC ROCK
00310058

CLASSICAL THEMES
00240160

CONTEMPORARY CHRISTIAN
00240245

COUNTRY HITS
00702013

NEIL DIAMOND
00702012

GOOD OL' SONGS
00240159

GOSPEL SONGS
00240143 ($8.95)

HYMNS
00240103

INTERNATIONAL FOLKSONGS
00240104

JAZZ STANDARDS
00240114 ($8.95)

BILLY JOEL
00240267

ELTON JOHN
00240257

LATIN SONGS
00240156

LOVE SONGS
00240150

MORE JAZZ STANDARDS
00240269

MOTOWN HITS
00240125

MOVIE MUSIC
00240113

POP/ROCK
00240179

ELVIS PRESLEY
00240102

ROCK & ROLL COLLECTION
00702020

RODGERS & HAMMERSTEIN
00240177

SOUL HITS
00240178

TV THEMES
00240170

FOR MORE INFORMATION, SEE YOUR LOCAL MUSIC DEALER, OR WRITE TO:

HAL•LEONARD®
CORPORATION
7777 W. BLUEMOUND RD. P.O. BOX 13819 MILWAUKEE, WI 53213

www.halleonard.com

0206

The PAPERBACK LYRIC COLLECTION
from HAL•LEONARD®

CHRISTMAS
Includes: All I Want for Christmas Is You • Auld Lang Syne • Away in a Manger • Baby, It's Cold Outside • Happy Xmas (War Is Over) • Hark! The Herald Angels Sing • Jingle-Bell Rock • Silver Bells • and more.
00240273 ....$7.95

THE 1950s
Timeless classics include: All Shook Up • At the Hop • Blue Suede Shoes • Blueberry Hill • Donna • Fever • Jambalaya (On the Bayou) • Misty • Peggy Sue • Rock Around the Clock • Splish Splash • Unchained Melody • Walkin' After Midnight • and more.
00240274 ....$7.95

THE 1960s
Classics include: All You Need Is Love • Beyond the Sea • California Dreamin' • Downtown • Hey Jude • It's My Party • Leaving on a Jet Plane • Louie, Louie • Respect • Stand by Me • Twist and Shout • more.
00240275 ....$7.95

THE 1970s
Favorites include: American Pie • Anticipation • Cat's in the Cradle • (They Long to Be) Close to You • Dust in the Wind • Fire and Rain • I Am Woman • Imagine • Reunited • Y.M.C.A. • You're So Vain • Your Song • and more.
00240276 ....$7.95

Visit Hal Leonard online at
www.halleonard.com

THE 1980s
Hits include: Another One Bites the Dust • Call Me • Candle in the Wind • Crazy Little Thing Called Love • 867-5309/Jenny • Every Breath You Take • Fast Car • Footloose • Hurts So Good • Legs • Longer • Missing You • and more.
00240277 ....$7.95

THE 1990s
Collection includes: All I Wanna Do • Beauty and the Beast • Black Velvet • Closer to Free • Come to My Window • Fields of Gold • Iris • More Than Words • Smells like Teen Spirit • Smooth • Tears in Heaven • Walking in Memphis • and more.
00240278 ....$7.95

THE 2000s
Today's hits, inc
Accidentally in Love •
These Hazel Eyes •
Hills • Breathe (2 AM) •
• Drops of Jupiter (T
The Middle • Mr. Bri
100 Years • Redneck
You Raise Me Up • ar
00240279 ....

3 1143 00791 6027

Prices, contents and availability are
to change without notice.
Some products may not be avail
outside the U.S.A.

FOR MORE INFORMATION, SEE YOUR LOCAL MU
OR WRITE TO:

HAL•LEONARD®
CORPORATION
7777 W. BLUEMOUND RD. P.O. BOX 13819 MILWAUKEE, WI 53213